DAD'S RULES FOR BEING A KICKASS ADULT

DAD'S RULES FOR BEING A KICKASS ADULT

Kevin L. Belzer

JONES MEDIA
PUBLISHING

Jones Media Publishing
10645 N. Tatum Blvd. Ste. 200-166
Phoenix, AZ 85028
www.JonesMediaPublishing.com

Printed in the United States of America

ISBN-13: 978-1-945849-55-8 paperback

DEDICATION

This book is dedicated to my three dad figures growing up:
Darrel Belzer, my father
Rodney Ward, my step father
And
Loyd Lafever, my grandfather
I have been blessed to learn many of the rules I will be

passing on in this book from these men.

Contents

PROLOGUE

WHEN I FIRST HAD THE idea for this book, I started from a very selfish standpoint. The initial idea was to write down my thoughts on what a kid needs to know before they enter the big old mean world of reality.

I planned on sharing them only with my kids. The idea of publishing them hadn't even crossed my mind. My oldest son was graduating from high school. I felt school had failed him and we, as parents, hadn't helped in giving him a complete blueprint of how to handle life outside of the comfort of our home.

He knew our home offered free room and board including Wi-Fi, Amazon Prime membership and a Netflix password. Reality of what else resided outside of our four walls was lost to him. Living in the burbs of Phoenix, we offered him a very Pollyanna lifestyle with little preparation.

This uneasy feeling went through me. It resembled one of disappoint in myself. It was a sense of failure in not teaching him everything he needed to be to live a productive and easier life.

I will never say that life is easy. It isn't. I will say that I needed to make sure it was easier for him to navigate it if I gave him the tools and the knowledge from my 40+ years on the planet.

Since I had met and interacted with humans, it would only make sense that I finally put to paper how I felt he could have the most productive life, the most fulfilling life possible.

For years, I have had these unwritten rules I lived by. When I sat down to map them all out, I realized that I had over forty of them. Some always had their place. They were unmoving. I could just say a rule number and people that knew me understood the rule. They became the unspoken ones.

Rule numbers 1, 3, 6 and 10 were this way.

I wanted this volume to cover what I felt are the essential ones to start with.

Included in this book are what I consider to be the foundation, the first ten. God-willing, I plan to write more volumes that will explore the others, but I felt it necessarily urgent to get the first ten out to all humans sooner rather than later.

I am not perfect. I know...shocking. Because of this, I will share the times I failed as well as what I learned to be better. A lot of the stories within are very personal and have never been shared before. I felt that it was important to show my flaws though so that you could see it is okay to start from wherever you are at. The journey towards a goal of being a better human can be quite enlightening.

These rules are in your face. It is intentional. Some may come across as harsh and I planned it that way.

Life is tough so I make no apology for the language contained within. I have done it to drive home the point of the rule being covered.

It may seem a little odd that I will drop a "naughty" word and then drop a Bible verse next. Please bear with me and read on. There is gold in the words sprinkled in between. I am a cursing Christian wearing my flaws for all to see.

If you are a parent, tone it down when explaining the rule. An example would be that instead of telling them to not be an asshole you tell them to not be a jerk, punk, or bully. Instead of telling them that patience is bullshit, tell them patience is tough or hard.

My goal out of this book is that we all apply the rules within and become better humans. All the rules are practical and apply to events happening throughout our day. The cursing is to wake you up and get you moving.

Like I said, I started this with selfish intentions. What I learned is that I can't be selfish about the rules within this book. Now more than at any time in our history, we could all benefit from these rules and make this world a better place.

I know that sounds crazy, but I challenge you to read this book and start applying it to your day.

Over the course of writing this, the rules were always on my mind. I found myself diving deeper and deeper into living them and sharing them with anyone that cared to listen. I watched a transformation in my life. I felt myself caring passionately about what really mattered. I found I liked myself more. Out of that, I saw it bleed over into other areas of my life from family to friends and even my career. Everything was more exciting and life became even more of a joy.

Every great change in history started with one person believing they could make a change. I believe that can be you.

> *He said to them, "Because of your little faith. For truly, I say to you, if you have faith like a grain of mustard seed, you will say to this mountain, 'Move from here to there,' and it will move, and nothing will be impossible for you."*
>
> *Mathew 17:20 (ESV)*

I throw down a challenge. Read this book and be the change this world needs. I believe you can read, then act on these rules and make your life and this world better. Hey, God believes you can do anything!

Now, on to Rule #1!

RULE #1)
DON'T BE AN ASSHOLE

"Did you ever think for a second, I'm only human too?"
taken from the song "You Don't Know"
by Kobra and the Lotus

HUH...SEEMS LIKE A NO brainer, right? Sadly, this is not the case.

I am a Real Estate Consultant by profession. I work with sellers and buyers. Back when the market crashed in 2007 and 2008, traditional buyers and sellers, people looking to live in a home or sell their primary residence, went into hibernation. For buyers, financing became very hard to attain. The pendulum had swung from "Everyone is approved" to over-scrutinizing of perfectly qualified buyers. We all understood changes needed to happen, but this wasn't the answer.

The traditional sellers got the brunt of this by having homes they couldn't sell because of the lack of qualified buyers. Meanwhile, the market starts to tumble. What starts as a simple correction in the market leads to parts of the Phoenix valley losing 75% of value into 2010.

So, what does this have to do with assholes, jerks, bullies, etc.?

Out of the ashes rise investors, both pro and amateur. At one time, I worked with these investors. Some of them are the reason I make this rule #1. All of them are looking to take advantage of a declining market. Did I, then or now, blame them? Nope.

I did, however, have issues with their attitudes.

What this declining market did was introduce me to a world of characters, both good and evil. While some appreciated my and my fellow agents expertise, many had sadly spent four hours at a seminar learning everything they needed to know about getting rich in the real estate market. This included anything from doing shoddy work or not paying an agent fair value for their time to people simply being in way over their heads.

I could write a book on the things that made me move on from working with different "investors", but will instead focus a few pages on one snippet of their character. One investor in particular represented a true asshole mentality.

From the moment I started working with them, I should have known better. I will admit that I too was blinded by the income potential of working with investors. They could do many projects at once, which would give me a steady stream of new homes to sell, as well as find more for their next project.

I negotiated my commission up from a low amount they thought my time was worth. I remember not being happy with it, but felt with the volume it would work out fine over time. What I didn't realize was the monopolization of my time they felt was now necessary since they were paying me more. Mind you, I was still going to be compensated below market value. That was irrelevant to them.

The phone would start ringing at 7am and go on throughout the day until 10pm. Most days, I would have upwards of 12-15 calls from each investor that were really about nothing or no value. I remember being told to go see if he turned the lights off at a house. If I were to question this, I would be threatened with losing the listing.

Any mistake on the project was my fault or the contractor or the market. Never did it fall on their shoulders. It was their money and they were, I thought, grownups so the decision to move forward, paint a home tan, add appliances, pick wood flooring over tile, it was all their decision to make. People need to be accountable. That was my opinion. I would advise but did believe, and still do believe, that they were responsible for what happened as a result of the decision.

Not to them though.

I remember bringing a project to an investor once and being berated about how it couldn't possibly make money.

Fine. I took it to another investor and another investor and yet another investor before one said okay to it. He made $177,000 on it after expenses. They all find out (because I told them, heh heh) and get pissed that I didn't push them harder. Really?

I should have known better the quality of people I was surrounding myself with (assholes) and moved on, but I didn't. I, for some reason, felt that it was their right to treat people this way because they had money. I know this logic makes no sense, but it was the first time in my life I was exposed to so much wealth.

What I was about to learn though was that we do all have a breaking point.

The final straw for me was when I was sitting at my office being yelled and screamed at over the phone for the umpteenth time about something that had nothing to do with me. I set my phone down with him still yelling, went to the bathroom, stopped by kitchen to get a bottle of water and then came back to the phone. He was still ranting.

I couldn't believe what I had done. It all just hit me at once that I was done being treated like this. I had that moment where enough was enough. I couldn't take the abuse anymore.

"Look, I can't do business with you anymore," I said.

"What are you talking about? Why not?" He fumed.

"I just don't need this abuse. I'm done," I replied.

I had spoken to my wife and told her I had never made so much money and been so miserable. It was true. In spite of the lower compensation, I was making good money. I was also working longer hours and getting zero respect for all I had done, such as fighting a low appraisal on one of their projects and getting increased by $16,000 by taking it all the way to the appraisal board for review. Never in my life had I popped so many antacids. It was as if they were candy!

He yelled," Do you know how much I am worth? I am worth over $20 million!"

"Yeah," I said," but you are still an asshole."

There it is. Can an asshole get their way?

Absolutely.

The real question is how long can they keep getting their way? At some point, people will have enough of their ways and be done.

I tapped out and it cost me immediate income for a few months. However, I had to think long term of what damage this asshole was doing to my sanity and health. No amount of money was worth the grief.

It drove home an important lesson to me personally. Don't be that guy. Money and wealth were things I strived for but I couldn't see doing it at the expense of my character.

If you were to describe yourself in one word, what would it be?

Strong, valiant, driven, exciting or emotional, sad, pathetic, asshole...the options can be from grand to poor. It is up to you to show the world what you are and what you radiate to them.

Do people perceive you as a light to the room or darkness? Do you drive people to excellence or do you make them feel worse? Is it a blessing you entered the room or a curse to all who come into contact with you?

Whether you like it or not, perception is a reality. You can think it is unfair that people think of you as a whiner, an asshole or a sad human being, but if that is the persona you give off then it is your fault.

Let's look at it another way. None of us starts from birth better than anyone else. Sure, some may be born into a wealthy family or have a marquee name at birth. That is different. We all have to learn and develop and decide what we want to make of ourselves and of our lives. Because that child was born into wealth or into a family with connections doesn't mean that they have any right to be an asshole.

Now, let's not let people born into poverty or lesser means be off the hook either for being immune to being an asshole. As there is no guarantee that a wealthy person will be an asshole, there can also be no way of guaranteeing that a poor person won't be one.

Let's think about this a little deeper. Have you ever met someone that treats someone like crap because they were born without the proverbial silver spoon in their mouth? They hate anyone with money and treat those like an asshole because they have what they don't or won't go after. How dare that rich person have money when I don't so I refuse to show him or her any respect! That is how they go about their day. Or, they look down on those around them with even less than they have.

The thing is, you can be an asshole whether you are rich or

poor, fat or skinny, male or female, regardless of race, religion or ethnicity. It is an equal opportunity for all to be an asshole.

Good news is that the choice is up to you on what you decide to be. The one word to describe oneself doesn't have to be asshole.

You have the power to show respect to your fellow man. You have the power to be better.

Be nice to the people you meet on the way up because they are the same ones you will meet if you go back down.

So what happened to the investor you may ask?

They were out of the game within 2 years. I don't know the details but I would be lying if I said it didn't give me some sense of happiness. Hey, I am not perfect...

He was an asshole. Don't be an asshole.

So, don't be so driven to win at any cost that you think being an asshole is okay. I have no issues with someone wanting to win, but at the destruction of your own character is unacceptable.

Being an asshole is a character trait that no one should be reaching or striving towards.

Imagine being eulogized at your funeral. I know, you will be dead so what do you care. Don't be a sarcastic asshole and just hear me out.

I have given a few eulogies over the years. What has always stuck with me is the character of the people I have eulogized. I have looked out over the services and spoken to packed rooms. So far, I have been blessed to only speak for those with high character and the good they brought to the world. Thing is, if they weren't good people, would I have even spoken at their services? Chances are close to zero percent.

People don't want to remember assholes. They want to move on from them. They are like a dirt or filth that need to be removed from the body as soon as possible. I know when I am around an asshole, I tend to need to read more to get my mind right. They are like a cancer. I also want to get away from them as soon as possible and find every reason to not work with them.

As I have spent more time as a Real Estate Agent, I find myself getting much more picky with those I work with. I won't work with assholes. I don't care if your home is sellable or not, I am not the right fit for you. Go find another agent that meshes with you better. My mental health is too important.

Being an asshole is detrimental to your success.

Sure, you may still get rich. There are lots of rich assholes on this planet. That isn't the success I am speaking of though. Getting rich and being an asshole will not give you true friends. It will have friends that only see a financial benefit to them. They will use you for personal gain.

Life needs to be more than that. You need to not only have great financial success but also surround yourself with true friends. God didn't make you to be alone. He designed us to be stronger together.

No matter where you are at financially, you owe your fellow humans kindness. Even if someone deserves to be treated in an asshole manner, you need to think big picture and ask yourself if this is a good idea. We will have more on this in future rules.

I saw a story recently that drove home this rule. Names have been changed.

Bob pulled into the parking garage. Another car took his spot and finished off the asshole maneuver by flicking Bob off and telling him to fuck off. That alone is bad enough. Dude, it is a parking spot. Don't be rude. Besides, the walk could be good for you!

So, Bob finds another spot. He goes in to work and is told that his first interview for the day, Chris, is there. Who should walk in but the same guy that flicked him off and told him to fuck off. Chris realized really quickly how small our world was and prepared himself for the most awkward interview of his life. Bob had a choice at that moment to call him out or let it go and interview him like any other candidate.

Bob treated him with respect and carried out the interview. He wouldn't have been looked down on by most of us for going with the other option, but Bob didn't think like everyone else. He was an exception.

I believe we can let an asshole ruin our day or move along. Even when I fired the asshole client, I wasn't letting him ruin my day. I was moving along to stop him from causing me any more grief. I believe Bob was doing the same thing. An asshole isn't worth the emotional luggage it carries with it.

Bob could have been looking at this as a moment of stress for the guy and not a normal asshole behavior. Chris was there for a job interview. Maybe he had been unemployed for months and the stress was getting to be more than he could bear.

We all have asshole moments. We aren't perfect. Stress can bring out inner demons. It is only a problem once it is a pattern. Benefit of the doubt is fine until then.

If you choose to be an asshole or lose your cool, don't expect people to be as understanding as Bob. Most people aren't that way. Most will dish out whatever you serve up. If you give people a shitty attitude, you should anticipate it is about to be thrown right back at you. Mirroring of attitudes, good or bad, should be expected.

However, if you give people kindness, seldom will they give back an attitude. Most people are good at heart. To believe otherwise is a cynical way to go through life. I know we have free will, but I have a hard time believing that if you give away good that you are going to get a majority of bad back.

That isn't to say you will never get bad back. There are bad people and assholes out there. The world is full of dark people. With that said, I still believe that if you give away good, it will come back to you in tremendously overflowing amounts.

I need to add a caveat to all of this.

You can be aggressive and demanding of others and not be an asshole. It is possible. I am in no way telling you to be light in getting what you want.

Some people mislabel a person with a strong personality as an asshole. That isn't necessarily the case. You can expect the best of others or want people to do their job and not be an asshole.

It can go down to the tone of voice you are conveying. I would hate to see anyone lumped into the asshole category undeservedly.

Here is perfect example that just happened this morning.

I knew from the agent's first few words this was a bad call. She asked how I was this morning, but I could tell by her tone of voice that it wasn't going to be an uplifting telephone call.

She was calling to cancel her client's deal on one of my listings.

I said to myself, in my head, she was going to cancel. Even as I answered, I was doing it well in response to her question.

Words mean things. We hear that as we are growing up.

Tone is even more valuable though.

What do I mean?

You can say things that are polite and friendly, but if your tone, like this agent's, is one that says they are sad and disappointed, my reception to you can or will be altered.

It is easy to fall into someone else's mindset if you let it and their tone shows you where they are at.

I had a sign call on a listing on Saturday. The guy's tone sounded like one of annoyance. He said he didn't expect someone to answer and he just wanted to know the price. I am unclear why he thought I wouldn't answer. That wasn't the direction of annoyance or sarcasm that I wanted or planned on giving back.

We can easily match tone if we aren't careful. If they are

conveying a tone of excitement and joy, those are easy and acceptable to give back. However, if they are feeding you sarcasm, annoyance, or anger, you have to be the better person and not fall into their tone. No one wins and no one gains in that situation.

When the client got annoyed at me for answering the phone, I smiled. My smile and helpfulness came across when I responded back with some information on the home. I was then able to learn more about his situation and what he needed out of a home. I could have blasted back with a witty amount of sarcasm. I am well trained in sarcasm. However, how would I have pushed society forward by being a jerk?

> **"If you run into an asshole in the morning, you ran into an asshole. If you run into assholes all day, you're the asshole." Raylan Givens, fictional character on TV series Justified.**

Let's get back to the agent.

The agent went over what was wrong with the home. I didn't get defensive. There wasn't a reason to do that. She had an inspection with photos. Her buyers wanted to walk away, which was their right. I wanted to have an honest conversation with the agent and see what were the main issues so I could convey them to my client and see if we could get them resolved for the next buyer who comes along.

This agent made it clear her buyers were going to walk so I couldn't save the deal but I could deliver a friendly tone and gain the insight necessary to hold a deal together the next time.

My tone to her was critical. I needed to be friendly. I was genuinely sad for her client and mine, but I needed to give a positive tone that this stuff happens and not all deals are meant to be. Without doing that, I would have no idea why they were planning to walk away, or at least, not the whole story. Being confrontational and showing anger towards her had no value.

How do you come across to others?

It really got me thinking about all areas of my business.

When I am prospecting, do I come across as someone that is happy to help or annoyed that they called? It seems funny that I would be annoyed that someone called. I had run into a lender recently that got annoyed when I called to check on the qualification of their client. Their client wrote on a listing of mine and the prequalification was incomplete. I was put off by this attitude. I took a step back and asked myself, do I ever do that?

When I present inspection results or a low appraisal, do I come across as someone determined to find a solution or as one waving the white flag, going into the fetal position in a corner and losing my mind?

When I go into a phone call, how do I sound? If my heart doesn't feel into making the calls at that moment, I have found many ways to get my brain right. Anything from working out prior to my call day, listening to or reading a good book, music that motivates me or just taking in a few moments of silence to recalibrate my brain.

Check your tone before you answer or make calls. I guarantee this is a game changer and will put extra money in your pockets.

I had a transaction years ago where the inspection was really bad. The electricity wasn't on when we looked at the home, but was turned on after the contract was accepted. During inspection, we found out that the power wasn't working in half the home. I ended up cancelling the deal. I remember telling the agent that it wasn't her fault. The bank owned it and wouldn't fix it. Nothing she could do about it. I wished that agent luck and moved my clients on to another home.

Fast-forward three years, a family came to me and wanted to buy their first home. The area they liked was very competitive. I showed them a home that was listed by this agent. We presented an offer and she said she remembered how I treated her on that other home. She said she would convey that story to her client to show my character as an agent. She did and my client got the home.

It is too easy to fall into other's bad days or the bad moments in front of us. Don't do it. It has zero return on investment. Complaining gets no one paid. Bad attitudes and bad tones toward others have zero value.

Human better and watch your tone. You never know when the returns will happen.

Said another way: Don't be an asshole.

RULE #2)
DON'T BE A DUMBASS

**"You don't have bad luck. The rea-
son that bad things happen to you
is because you're a dumbass."
Father of the year, Red Forman, That 70s Show**

THERE IS A DIFFERENCE BETWEEN making mistakes in
life and being a dumbass. There is wisdom in Red's words.

Tell me, what scenario has ever ended well when prefaced
with the following:

"Hey, hold my beer."

Or-

"I double-dog dare you!!!"

Let me make something very clear that needs to be conveyed
to the young ones at a very early age. When Tommy or Gina
double-dog dare you to do anything, you are NOT OBLIGATED

by cosmic rules to do said double-dog-dared activity.

Should we humans be adventurous?

Absolutely!!!

However, when the voice inside your head is saying that something isn't a good idea, it may be wise to listen to it.

That voice is either mom saying, "Maybe that isn't a good idea." Or, it's dad saying, " Hey! Don't be a dumbass!"

Now why, oh why, would dad say it in such a harsh way?

The shock of his words, are meant to snap the child into making a common sense decision, and to not move forward with the dumb-assery of the current challenge they were probably double-dog dared into doing.

I have put dumbass on display many times over the years. Being a dumbass can affect you in many ways. You can have financial hardship, pain, lost trust, and even death as a result of being a dumbass.

One time, I was driving the family back from Christmas at grandma's house. I loved going to Grandma's and loved even more that my kids could get exposed to such a woman of intellect and caring. She truly had a servant heart. On this trip, we took a few extra days, got nice and refreshed from all that relaxing. There is nothing quite like a long weekend of home-cooked meals, pies, and freshly churned ice cream to make you appreciate life.

Like most of our trips, I preferred to leave in the evening time. Traffic was lighter and we got more time with the family. Plus, the kids will sleep on the drive home. We said our goodbyes, put our two kids into the backseat, and headed down the highway on our 4-hour drive. All was right with the world.

It was like a switch flipped inside of me as we hit the highway. I had to go fast and had to be first. My first gaming console was the Atari 2600. We had this game called Pole Position. The goal of any racing game is to win. My problem was that I felt this way on the road as well. I needed to be ahead of whatever car was in front, as they were CLEARLY not driving fast enough, even if they appeared to others to be setting land speed records.

Sure, I would tell myself that I didn't want to be the "Rabbit". That was the car going the fastest. Theory was that they would be the one spotted by the cop and give me enough warning. They got pulled over and I continue on my way in hopes of another rabbit to set the pace. The problem was, my relatively young punk ass could get amped up.

We made it around the south suburbs of Chicago. The weather over the past hour had gotten progressively worse. We went from clear skies to this wet mist as well as a temperature drop. I knew all this but had this underlying road rage burning up my insides from all the HORRIBLE drivers around me.

How dare they not understand that these roads are MINE? They should clear out of my way leaving me free passage all the way home to my castle.

"Oh! You want me to get over because I am not going FAST enough? Eff off, mother effer! I will effing show you a speed you can't tailgate! I will effing show YOU!"

This car cuts me off. I gun the gas and whip to the left and around him. As I get in front of him his headlights are lighting up the interior of my car. There is no way he won't see my one finger salute as I let him know, that yes, he is number one and can eff off!

Karma happened. A true "God smack" through the hood of my car down to those front wheel driven tires made it known that I had crossed the line.

The car hit a sheet of black ice and spun around on the highway. We were now going backwards at over 60 miles per hour, finally ending in a ditch facing the opposite direction, where after several hundreds of feet we slammed to a stop. We avoided hitting any other vehicles in this free spin amongst semi-heavy traffic. We only cracked a taillight cover from hitting the one sapling to be seen in the ditch for miles.

My wife has said she has only heard me make a sound of fear and terror twice in her life. This was one of those times. I look in the backseat and see Zach and Mac awake now, wondering what just happened.

My dumbass moment could have killed them.

I knew I was a dumbass. I was telling myself in my head that I was so stupid. I let ego and rage take hold of me. Here I was, in a position of responsibility, not making responsible decisions. Those two kids and my wife had all been sleeping. They were entrusting me with the job of getting them home safely.

I took everything I had learned about enjoying life and those around me at grandma's house and threw it out the window as soon as I hit the highway.

I was a true, clear as day, dumbass at that moment.

THINK

So, you don't want to be a dumbass? Start with this simple five-letter word

THINK

Think first before doing something you may regret for the rest of your life. Though I don't believe it is healthy to look back on life with regrets, I do know that we all have moments we wish we could take back. We have those moments we wish we could undo.

I like to think I am pretty smart, but I know I have had many times in the past that a few extra seconds, minutes or even days would have saved me months or years of grief or financial pain. I should have looked at the whole picture and analyzed the long-term consequences.

If you are feeling pressured into making a decision that your inner voice is fighting, it may not be a bad idea to take a step back. That doesn't mean, though, that doing it is a bad decision. You may just need a few more facts. Growth will have pain involved so don't always believe you should do nothing.

For this next story, these kids definitely should have stayed home and played video games instead.

In 2014, 62 students were arrested after breaking into their school, Teaneck High School in New Jersey, after hours. It doesn't stop there though. They decided that it would be a good idea to pee all over the hallways, ransack the classrooms and throw around some balloons and streamers.

That is a total dumbass move that had permanent consequences. This school knew who did it and pressed charges. Doing something at this level of stupidity forever altered the rest of their lives.

It should be common sense, but let me state it anyway. Don't do anything that will get you arrested. You may be a dumbass if you get arrested.

Actually, you are a dumbass if you get arrested. No "maybe" about it...

We joke about the "Hold my beer." moments, but they really aren't a joke. These moments end up being lessons that started with someone not thinking before doing.

I believe, it is better to witness and learn from the "Hold my beer" people than to actually be the "Hold my beer" person.

Let's make this next point clear: Spontaneity in life is awesome!

Don't, for a moment, think that I don't want you to be spontaneous. Life should be lived epically. I will have more on that in a later rule.

What I am talking about here is common sense. What could I have done differently on that drive home? I could have put some music on. I could have woken up my wife and talked to her. I could have pulled off the road and cleared my head. I should have done anything other than what I did.

I learned a valuable lesson that day, but it could have cost me my family. I got lucky. We aren't always so lucky. We can't always undo bad moments.

ASK

If you are wondering if an idea is sound, ask for counsel. You aren't expected to have all the answers, but if you move forward on a questionable business decision without seeking counsel from others, you may be making a dumbass decision.

I have a coach in my real estate business. It is the best thing I ever added into my business. Sometimes, we are too close to see what is really going on. When you are playing with millions of dollars, mistakes are amplified. You will never get to that level if you don't first learn to not be a dumbass in the hundreds or thousands. Experience gained and knowledge learned will be invaluable in showing you how easy it is to play in the hundreds of thousands and millions in production.

I have made some stupid business decisions with no counsel. I have gotten counsel on others that I ended up choosing to move forward with as well as set aside others when I got that don't be a dumbass look. I wish I had gotten advice on all of them. If someone tells you it is a now or never moment, you can tell that person nicely that you will have to pass.

Or…tell them to eff off. You be the judge.

Now, that said, you need to make sure the advice is coming from a good place and they are really knowledgeable about what they are telling you.

For example, don't take financial advice or make a financial decision based solely on the advice of someone with no money. Hey, they may know what they are talking about, but I would want another opinion. They may be on to something huge but there may also be a reason that they are broke. They may be full of shit.

I know what you are thinking. If I don't know, how do I "sniff through the bullshit"? I will admit, that could be tough but let's start with some basics.

Do they truly have your best interest at heart or are they trying to hold you down because down is safe? Are they advising you to pull you up to their level of success or keep you down in their misery where they can control you?

Don't misunderstand. I think the world is full of awesome loving people. To think all people are out to get you simply isn't a healthy way to live. That being said, I do know the world has a mix of evil and good in it.

When I started my job as a Real Estate Agent, I was told by all but one person that I was stupid for giving up my security. What was I doing getting into an industry that had houses dropping thousands of dollars in value a day? No one was buying! Those who wanted to sell couldn't sell. Besides, I was 36 years old. I needed to think of the kids and grow up. What was I doing starting a new career?

My sister-in-law, who I have known since she was 14, was the only one that said to go for it. She came from a different angle. She said if I could survive in this market, I would crush it when the market turned around. No market stays down forever.

She was right. This wasn't a dumbass decision. In fact, this could possibly be the perfect time to get into Real Estate. Did I go through a lot of trials the first couple years? Yes, I did.

However, I learned so much about sales while overcoming objections and got paid for all the training and skills I was learning.

I also made sure I had a mentor to save me from making bad decisions. Now, that doesn't mean I always listened. It did take me a little while to listen with both ears.

LISTEN

It is one thing to ask for others opinions concerning business, but a totally different thing to actually be listening to their advice.

I am as guilty as the next person with this.

"What do you think of this car?"

"It's cool."

"I think I am going to buy it."

"Yeah? How much are the payments?"

"I don't know. I think like $500."

"$500! Wow! Can you afford that?"

"Oh yeah. I mean, if they keep giving me overtime, I am totally good to go. It will be tight but, you know, I work hard and I deserve this. Besides, they have it in red and I love red."

"So, what happens if they cut the overtime?"

"Oh, I would be totally screwed!" I laugh.

" Seriously, what happens?"

"Oh, I don't know. I will figure it out. They say I won't have a payment for like 45 days so if I put that in the bank, I will have a cushion if anything happens."

"How much you got saved now?"

"Like $5, but I can do it."

"You probably shouldn't do it. Your car runs fine. You just need to wash it and it is good as new."

"Yeah...but, they have it in red and I like red. I am going to do it."

"Don't do it!"

"Yeah...kind of too late. I already did it."

Dumbass.

Shiny-object syndrome. I really believe this is a thing. We have something perfectly fine and we go and get something newer and shinier to replace it. No wonder we have so much debt as a society.

Shiny-object syndrome leads to debt. Debt is one of the side effects of being a dumbass. Rather than save for something, we need to have it now.

If that inner voice is telling you not to do it, whether it is buying that new car or your 40th pair of shoes, you should probably pause and see if it is makes sense to go forward with your purchase.

Listening to a coach or mentor who you look up to can save you from many mistakes. It can also accelerate your success. If others have "been there, done that", why are you ignoring them? The only time to take it in stride and not as gospel is when it isn't duplicable.

If my coach came to me and told me how he helped a

lottery winner buy a $5 million house, I have nothing to learn from that. You can't duplicate it. It isn't like that is a market rich in buyers. I will just congratulate him and move along to something we can work with.

If he shows me a marketing campaign that generates 3 quality leads a day that are ready to buy, I will definitely listen because I can run with that campaign. It is something I can follow.

FOLLOW

I have asked for and listened to advice given by my mentor and coach in Real Estate. It has made me a fortune by following the advice. I had a choice. I could have listened to this successful person and instead done the opposite. That would have made me a dumbass for sure. I decided it would be the smartest, to not only ask and listen, but to also follow the advice.

You see, the advice is only good if it is followed by action. You don't want to seek advice from pros and just toss it aside. That is just plain dumb and you are way better than that.

To this day, I turn to a business partner and seek advice on everything from how to be a better agent to market analysis. I never think I know it all. Only a dumbass thinks they have nothing left to learn.

We regress into dumb-assery when we think we know it all. I like to look at everyday as an opportunity to get better, learn more, and have a positive impact on my fellow humans.

None of us is perfect. I, certainly, am not. The fact that this book has a proofreader and an editor is a clear indication of my lack of perfection. We all have dumbass moments. The goal is to not only minimize them but to minimize the potential damage that can occur as a result. I believe the next rule: Is this the hill you want to die on?, will further help you in not being a dumbass.

RULE #3)
IS THIS THE HILL YOU
WANT TO DIE ON?

Flee the evil desires of youth and pur-
sue righteousness, faith, love and peace,
along with those who call on the Lord out
of a pure heart. Don't have anything to
do with foolish and stupid arguments, be-
cause you know they produce quarrels.
(2 Timothy 2:22-23 NIV)

I AM NOT LETTING THIS car cut me off, I thought.

I glanced over, gave my car a little more gas. They should know to get over. Their lane ends at the railroad tracks. It is CLEARLY marked out!

I gave the car more gas. I had to be going close to 20 mph

over the posted limit. I knew at this point, I was going to win. I would beat them to the tracks. I, was once again, proven that I was better. They, in turn, were better for having me around to show them how to handle a merge situation.

I expected her to thank me. Instead, I could see in my rearview mirror that she was yelling.

Some people just aren't very grateful.

I drove back to the pizza place, grabbed my pizza bags and headed inside. It wasn't even two minutes later when she came into the store as well. I saw her, but I wasn't worried. I knew I was right. My manager was smart. She would see it my way.

The lady got so dramatic. She said that I could have killed her and her unborn baby. My manager listens to her story. I tell mine as well but forget that speeding is a moving violation.

Though I felt the lady was wrong, I was as well. I broke the law.

Crap! I broke the law. Well, maybe it would be okay. In my head, I tried to figure out if this was salvageable at all.

The manager said she had no choice. I was suspended. She said I was lucky I wasn't fired.

Though I try to not look back on life with regrets, I do have quite a few moments that could have been better handled by following rule #3.

This rule will be a double-edged sword, of sorts. I find in my day-to-day life asking this question multiple times a day!

That is why it is my favorite rule.

This rule can have the biggest impact on your life. It can correct mistakes before they happen. It can alter the direction your life takes for the better. It will make you a better human.

Is that too much? Is that a little over the top? I don't think so.

It must be decided if what you are about to say or do is for the good. You must decide whether it is just for your benefit or those around you. Will it progress that which needs to be accomplished or is it not important at all?

It must also be decided if it may have life-altering consequences for the better. Quitting a job or getting yourself fired may seem to others like insanity, but I strongly disagree if it is backed by logical thought prompted by this rule. Is the job, which you are at, a dead-end? Will it get you to your end goal? Is there a benefit to you, in being around the people working there, advancing you towards your dream?

Hey, that may seem selfish, but it's not! Life is too short to work a crappy job or career. If after breaking it all down, and coming to the conclusion that the best solution is to "die on this hill", then do it! God bless you for having the courage to realize before spending your whole working life in misery!

A little document called the Declaration of Independence states that you have a right to the pursuit of Happiness. I happen to fully agree with a hardy "Huzzah!!!"

Quitting a job or career is a major decision and shouldn't be taken lightly. Thought should go in to the pros and cons. One should also think about whether they can transition out with the new opportunity on the side. Think about this: If after weighing it all out, you come away with an emphatic "YES" when asking yourself if this is the hill, then go forth and die valiantly.

I had a job years ago that I worked 2 ½ days. I was sitting in my car, on day three, eating my lunch. I had some hair metal playing in the background, my thinking music for most major decisions in my life. I asked myself a pretty simple yet heavy question.

"What am I doing here?" My inner voice asked.

Wow. Ok. I guess I need some money.

"Yeah, but why here?"

Ooh, that is a good question. Why was I here? Of all places, why had I chosen this place?

It's close to home, I told myself.

"So what? Why does that matter?"

Huh...

I...uh...I got nothing, I told myself.

"Ok. So, do you like it here?"

No. Here it is only my 3rd day and I don't want to go back in after lunch. I seem to be the only one working as others stand around watching. That kind of... No, that DEFINITELY, pisses me off. Plus, the job is not challenging to my intelligence at all! I am getting nothing out of this.

"Ok, then quit. "

Really?

"Yeah. Just quit."

But, the money...

"Really? 3 days in has the money become that much of a hold on you? Can you really not afford to move on? Life is too short to have a crappy job. I am sure, if push came to shove, you could find another crappy job. These seem to be everywhere, like cockroaches."

Ok. I am sold.

I turned the engine on, put it in drive and left. I didn't even go back inside. For sanity's sake, I decided I would "die on this hill."

Every action we take will have a consequence. Many are simple. You are thirsty, take a drink and thirst is quenched. Tired? Go to sleep and feel rested.

Some we don't even think about. Breathing, for example, is an action that we take for granted. We sure notice it when we have a cold and the nose is stuffed up. Have your head dunked in the pool and you think about it a lot.

These aren't what I want to cover here though. Let's talk about the actions we take that will define moments in time.

When I quit that job, I had to be okay with the action I was taking. I had to understand that if I drove away, the job, the income, and the results of my actions would be the "hill I died on." I had to understand that there were no take-backs, no do-overs or mulligans. I had to be completely at peace with my actions.

Quitting a job is a major fork-in-the-road moment. Though it came across as a flippant response on my part, quitting after

2 ½ days, it wasn't.

I believe tomorrow is never guaranteed. We have no promise of going to sleep and waking tomorrow. Since I believe in God, I am at peace with this and what could otherwise be an overwhelming reality.

What if you would approach every moment in your life and ask yourself, "Is this is the hill I want to die on?"

Say you get in a disagreement with someone. For instance, you know you are right and they are wrong. You KNOW in your soul that Bon Jovi is better than Motley Crue. What if you stepped back and asked yourself, "Is this the hill I want to die on?"

This example may seem silly, but is it really? We get in so many disagreements with our fellow humans. Most are petty like this. We blow them up and out of proportion. Names are called. Things are said that can't be unsaid. Feelings are hurt. Pain is caused and all because our band is better than theirs...

STOP!!!

What if you just moved on? In the big scheme of life, this moment is irrelevant. It has no value at all but to piss off others.

Let's say that you work in sales or a retail environment. We hear the expression all the time that the customer is always right.

Let me tell you a little secret. The customer isn't always right. In fact, they are wrong an awful lot.

But, even though they are wrong, I don't need to disagree with them. There is no value in that scenario. I will lose the sale. I may win the battle but I just lost the war because I died on the wrong hill.

Do you think you are more likely to win someone over with sugar or vinegar? You can take whatever they say and agree while turning it into the direction you want or need them to go.

Some will say I am manipulating them. That isn't the case at all. What I am actually doing is directing them to where they need to be in order to best help them WITHOUT hurting their feelings or making a fool out of them.

Everyone wants to be right all the time. It is simply not possible. What is possible, though, is the chance for you to human better and not embarrass them.

Here is an example of how to handle one.

"Hey Carol, you make a great point. I like where you are going with your idea. What if we tried such and such instead? Do you think that could get us the results we need?"

I can look back and think of all the meaningless crap I have cared about and argued over. I can think of how walking away or letting things go would have been of benefit down the line.

When that lady wanted to merge, I should have let her. I was less than a mile from the store. Would I have lost anything from letting her in? I was annoyed she didn't merge until the last few hundred feet, but annoyance isn't an excuse for what I did. I was being petty.

Move along from the petty. You are better than that.

Pettiness is never a hill to die on. Nobody wins.

Oh, your ego will say otherwise, but remember rule #1:

Don't be an asshole.

I believe we owe our fellow humans kindness. Being an asshole is picking the wrong hill. Though you 'won' the argument, did you really win anything or did you just lose the war?

I lost a week of income due to dying on the wrong hill. I also lost the respect of my manager and fellow employees. This happened 13 years ago. It took me probably five years to admit to myself, and to others, that I was wrong. It did have an affect in the direction my life took.

That is all minor compared to what could have been lost. I could have caused an accident. It seems I learn a lot from past driving mistakes...

I have had many times in my real estate career where I have had to ask myself if this is the hill to die on. Petty shit comes up throughout a transaction. I have to decide if these are worth fighting about and then I realize over and over again that the decisions I make, the actions I take will not only affect me but the client.

It gets even more humbling when you start to understand that your actions can effect others for the positive or for the negative.

I am in a business that, sometimes, has people that don't really know what they are doing. I am sure that is a lot of careers, now that I think of it.

Because of their inexperience, the people not knowing how to do their job tend to put strain on the rest of us. I have a few options available.

As a first option, I can let them know that they are morons. In the moment, I would be satisfied by this response to their tomfoolery. It would give me some immediate gratification. I would feel super smart for letting them know that, by their presence, they are making society a horrible place. I would clearly be helping them, by letting them know about something they are not capable of seeing because of their stupidity.

Well, not really.

This would be personal machismo gained at the expense of a fellow human being. It would be an asshole move.

As a second option, I could just let the stupidity pass. If I see it has no harm to the scenario in front of us, it won't really matter. I can nod my head or give an "Uh huh" over the phone and move along. Hey, if no harm is to be had, then why die on this hill?

As a third option, I can try and help them out. I only need to do this when it matters though. Again, be careful about where you focus your caring. The things that don't matter need to stay in the "don't matter" pile. Don't go rummaging in there thinking you have some gems or diamonds in there. You need to look at the "don't matter" pile as holey socks or used tissues. You need to look at them as stuff you will never bring back into your house or life again.

Got it?

Be careful on this one. Option three needs to be practiced only if necessary.

You use this when it is critical to the task at hand. In my business, if I need a document that they don't understand or just don't want to deal with it, I may try a tactic like this example:

"Hey, I know this document seems silly. I agree with you. If it were up to me, we would just forget about it. I have a broker that will want this. Yours probably will as well. I don't know about you, but, I want to get paid and I am not getting paid without it. How about I draw it up and have it signed on my end? Once I get it done, I will shoot it over for your clients to sign as well."

I am deflecting there. I am not telling him he is being a dumbass. I am trying to solve the problem in a diplomatic way. I am not dying on the hill, mind you. I am nudging him along.

Now, if he won't cooperate after that, I will have no choice but to escalate things and die valiantly. That would clearly be option four, dying on the hill.

I have had a recent case where I had to ask my client to trust me as I chose a hill to die on.

We were under contract on a home. The home was absolutely gorgeous. It was a classis mid century style home that had been upgraded without losing it's original 1940s charm. Everything was great until the home inspection.

A lot of the findings were minor but one major issue came up. It needed a new roof. We let the seller's agent know. Her client offered a credit that wouldn't cover the roof. The inspector said it showed signs of leaking all over the attic.

We said no. They offered a higher credit. It still wasn't enough and the lender wouldn't allow that large of a credit anyway. I told them we wanted the roof replaced. They said no.

We were at a crossroads.

I went to the buyer and asked her what she wanted. She said she wanted a roof. I told her that they were refusing but I would ask one more time.

I went back to the agent and she said they would do a credit and to take it or leave it.

I had a choice to make. This hill would cost her a home but I had a feeling they were bluffing.

I asked my client to trust me. I told her one of two things would happen. We either get a roof or she knows they meant it and we move on.

I sent in a cancellation.

Within an hour, my phone rang. They wanted to know if they did the roof, would we not move forward with the cancellation. My client said yes and we closed on it two weeks later with a new roof.

The correct "hill" was chosen. Choosing to ignore that battle and pushing for closing on her home without it getting repaired would have cost my client thousands of dollars in additional cost after closing. That would definitely have not been an acceptable outcome.

I have chosen to care less about a lot of stuff in life. I do care about people but I choose my battles very differently now.

Dying on every hill for so many years cost me so much

heartache and anxiety. I may have single-handedly kept Tums in business with all the antacids I consumed.

As the years have gone on, I have looked back and realized I fought the wrong "battles" and lost the "wars."

Stop thinking you are the answer to all of the world's ills and that you are going to solve everything. I wish the hours existed to solve it all. I wish I could care about everything. I have come to the realization that this simply isn't possible and I am okay with that.

I am not saying to not care at all. What I am saying is, focus on what you really care about. Delegate your heart to the things that matter most to you.

Pick your battles in life. Always take a moment to ask, is this the hill worth dying on?

Give your cares and your battles to moments and causes that matter to you and those you are trying to help. Imagine if you stopped spreading yourself so thin and focused your energy on what REALLY mattered to you?

What would that world look like?

If you don't care about professional basketball, stop watching it. Use that time for something that moves you. If you don't care about calculus in college, don't take it. If you don't care about who is dating who then stop getting dragged into the conversation or feigning interest. If you really don't want to talk politics then scroll on in your Facebook news feed.

These are the hills not worth dying on. Find your passions and give them your concern and let the small or meaningless things to you go away.

Life is way too short to spend time dying on other people's hills or dying for the wrong causes.

Live a meaningful life.

Die valiantly on the hills that are worth it.

RULE #4)
SHIT HAPPENS

Now we see things imperfectly, like puz-
zling reflections in a mirror, but then we
will see everything with perfect clarity. All
that I know now is partial and incomplete,
but then I will know everything complete-
ly, just as God now knows me completely.
1 Corinthians 13:12

I HATE TO SAY IT, but I have to.

Shit happens.

In Back to the Future, it happened first to Biff Tannen. Or so we thought. We see that it had been happening to his family throughout history. They were the bad guys so there is a sprinkling of karma with shit happening.

Do you know that you can do everything right and shit will

still happen to you? It sucks. It REALLY sucks and doesn't seem fair.

Here is what The Billy Graham Evangelical Association said in an article titled When Bad Things Happen, published January 27th, 2010:

It often feels like difficult circumstances are directed at us. We live in an imperfect world, and the Bible says that it rains on the just and the unjust. We all live through painful and uncomfortable things. Who are we trusting when those things happen to us? Are we self-reliant or do we rely on God? If we reach out to God in time of need, then we are accessing the One who created the universe. The Bible says that He is waiting for our response. He has already made the invitation through His Son Jesus. Why you? Because He loves you. He wants you to look to Him so He can rescue you and bring you peace.

You know what? Life isn't fair. It isn't cosmically balanced for one and all. We all make our way through it in a different way. Some of us will be blessed where it seems like all is well and live a life of perfectly balanced bliss.

At least, that is the appearance.

I say it appears that way because we all have different levels of shit to wade through. When you see success, I need you to understand something very important. You are witnessing the end result. You are seeing a story from the outside. You are seeing the effects of blood, sweat and tears poured into creating the end result. That end result may have taken years, but our brains will focus on what is and not what was.

Did you know even the wealthy get sick? I know...shocking. Even they have sadness and setbacks. Don't think that money can solve all problems. Now, it can probably take care of 80% of them but that still leaves 20% that will require some level of human interaction, problem solving skills or a good attorney.

So, life is a bitch.

It comes with pain, sadness, heartbreak, etc. It has a ton of potential baggage with it.

Isn't that awesome?

What? You think I am crazy for saying that, don't you? Maybe a little, but let's dive into why all this pain, sadness, heartbreak, and on and on, is okay.

Success doesn't happen in a vacuum. As much as this fast paced world wants us to believe we can wake up tomorrow skinnier, faster, stronger and wealthier, it simply isn't that easy. Obstacles will always come up. Things must be overcome. Our own minds will try and persuade us that it isn't possible to make it through the shit storm of life but I am telling you, it is possible. That shit you are going through, whatever it is, can make you stronger. It may not seem like it at the time and I won't discount the pain and heartache you will go through. I will say this though. Go through it. Don't sit in it and rot away.

Go through it and help the next human along to get through it.

If your life never had any difficulty along the way, how does that make you feel?

On the surface, pretty awesome! I mean, you may think to yourself that because of this you have success and fame and everybody loves you. No one ever challenges your opinion or makes you critically think because life is perfect.

Wait a second. I have no conflict, and no one makes me critically think? I have no challenges at all? How can anyone know how awesome I am if I never get to show them I am up to the challenge?

Where is the fun in that?

Life should have challenges and a competitive side to it.

The challenge of conquering the day drives me. I feel like I am in a battle to win hearts and minds to my side. In real estate, you either get your offer accepted or you are last. It isn't like they give you a back up house as a parting gift.

I look at that loss and, yes, I have disappointment because shit happened. I lost. I then ask myself what I can do better. What can I do to put my client in a better situation? If they don't have the highest offer, what can I do to convince the other side that I am still the best person to help you?

I had a transaction years ago where we were 1 of 29 offers. We were also the lowest of 29 offers. I could sit back, let my client lose the home or I could find a way to overcome this issue. The challenge was figuring out how to convince them to accept my offer when 28 others were better.

I had other offers not get accepted for this investor. I was tired of the shit happening again and again. The client and I had run the numbers and knew that the offer, even though it was the lowest, it was the best offer.

The house had continually fallen out due to bad inspections. I took a contractor by and had him look the house over. We had a very good idea of what it would cost to repair the home and make a profit. I called the agent and did what no other offer was willing to do. I waived the inspection period.

Our offer got accepted. We closed on the home, did the remodel, and sold it for a profit.

I had a choice. I could accept that shit happens over and over or I could take the past experiences and learn from them. This allowed me to move on from a position of losing to one of winning.

It is funny. Since then, I have looked at every transaction differently. I don't care how many offers are on a house. I don't care what the obstacles are. I am going to figure out a way to make it work or move on.

Shit can't happen in a controlled environment like that once you take command of it and let it know you are in charge.

Now, there is some shit that I wish on no one, like the loss of one's parents, but when it happens, you have a choice in how you react to it.

When my mother died, it tore me up. She died due to complications resulting from brain surgery and the after care. It pissed me off. It made me feel life is truly unfair. I hated that those doctors and nurses could be so careless with my mom.

It also made me think.

What did I think of my mom? I loved her. She was the most awesome mom anybody could wish to have. She was kind. She thought of others first. She loved to laugh. She was a great listener.

Wow. She was a role model. This dying shit really pissed me off, but it also drove home a major point. Be like her. Go forward showing the world what she taught me and pass that on.

I had a choice. I could move forward with a pissed off view of the world and how it treated me unfairly, or I could accept that it happened. Shit happened. I could learn from this, take the best of this shitty situation, and rise above to be better because of it. It is some really heavy shit, and it sucks, but I have to focus on how I will handle this moving forward.

And, moving forward, I wanted to remember her for being awesome. I wanted to remember what she taught me and pass that on instead.

We all go through grief. I am not discounting that at all. It is a natural emotion that we inevitably must confront. At some point, though, we need to move forward. It is how we choose to deal with that shit that will define us long term.

We also will have shit happen in our jobs. I have been fired a few times. My kids and I sat down and counted all the places I have worked and it was over thirty. They think that is crazy. I look at it and see it in many different ways. One is that shit just happens. Some jobs I quit, others I got fired. So what. It was all an experience. I also had some business ideas and ventures not take off the way I had hoped.

With the business ventures, I can look at the money and time spent on them failing and get pissed off. I have dropped $100k in to one to not see a dime of return as of this writing. I can look at another and get mad at the bank for not agreeing to loan me the capital.

This is shit that isn't totally in my control though. With the bank, I have no idea what goes through their minds but I can tell you, in hindsight, my presentation was weak. I blamed them for it at the time, not realizing, that to get the pitch opportunity was a huge deal. I blew the pitch. I have learned how to be a better presenter over the past several years and know, if I still had interest in that venture now, I could convince them to loan me the money. Looking back, I am glad they said no. My heart wasn't in it and time has moved on to where I would rather focus elsewhere.

With the one that I have sunk so much money in, I have chosen to look at it as a valuable learning experience. I can make the money again. I believe it is going in a positive direction now. I learned so much on what to do and what not do. I learned the value of research. I also learned, that I can't control keyboard warriors. I can't control people that are out to sabotage by pretending to be friends.

It is all good. I believe in rising above rather than sinking to someone else's level. I know that if we keep pushing on in the new direction it is going, that we will have the last laugh and that is one of success.

You see, shit happens in the business world. So what. Learn and move on. Take your lumps and push on. The negativity and shit only has an effect when you quit.

How I dealt with the firings is important as well. I was working at a pizza place and got fired. I deserved it. I didn't think so at that time, but in hindsight, I really did. I hardcore earned it. If they gave trophies for shit deserving to occur, that would have won first place.

I had to make a decision. Do I go to another pizza place, pick a different path, or sit and whine about it. This shit that happened to me was a huge deal. Our income went to zero. That was, no bueno. Bills don't get paid with zero money.

Within a few weeks, my wife ran across an ad posted in a Walmart for a job doing courier work. I called and got the job. Fast forward a few years, it led to an opportunity in Arizona. We left Indiana and headed to Phoenix. No snow. 300 days of sunshine.

So, shit happened. I lost a job. I got a new job that led us to move to a state where we had always wanted to live.

Once we got to Arizona, my wife gave birth to our third child. At the time, I was again between jobs. At that moment, we could stress and complain or we could trust God. I had applications in with a couple of jobs. While we were waiting patiently (yeah...right) for the birth to happen, unbeknownst to me, two jobs called me back and were leaving me messages.

One was during the day and one was at night. I figured we

could use the cash so I ended up taking them both. I had no idea how much both would help me down the line when I went into real estate. One job was as a courier. I drove all over Phoenix and surrounding area every day. I really learned the valley. The other job was delivering pizzas. Through that job, I met a co-worker who told me about this real estate company that would train me. He thought I would be good at it. I ended up taking a job with that company and eventually left with a few of the top agents to form the company, Go Sold Realty.

So, shit happened, but look where it led me?

Some see shit. I see manure fertilizing my future opportunities.

I wasn't always like this.

I went through my angst years, believing that the world was unfair only to me. It somehow singled me out making my life harder.

I am nowhere near perfect.

It took me years to realize that I was looking at the shit happening to me in the wrong way.

My parents divorced when I was just 2 years old. From any angle, one could say that really sucks. I could feel sorry for myself. I could wonder what I did wrong. It didn't matter that I was only two when it happened. The facts are that I was there. I could be the reason why they aren't together. This isn't the least bit logical, but who cares?

What if I flipped the script?

Both of my parents divorced. Whatever happened to lead to

that conclusion, well, it is too late to change it. Shit happened and we must move on. Where are we now? They both got remarried. I got more brothers and a sister. I learned and made memories with all these new people.

How awesome is that!

I could choose to cry, whine, or throw a pity-party. Yep. The world would say I had a RIGHT to be upset. Yeah, I could live in this negative mindset or I could move forward.

That is the easy way.

Let's try a harder way but a more rewarding one.

So, you are going through something right now that you think is not fair. It is a level of shit that no one should have to endure. You don't think I could possibly understand, for a moment ,the bullshit it is.

Let me tell you, what you are going through may not be something I could totally understand. We are unique and have different experiences.

With that said, we can all find a light at the end of the tunnel when we start looking for it.

Whatever you are going through, whatever shit has hit the fan, whatever pain you are going through, understand you are not alone.

What did I learn from all those jobs, bad business ventures, and cars breaking down when you are broke?

I learned I wasn't a slave to that moment. I didn't have to stay in it. I could choose to stay in it, but I didn't have to. I could rise above whatever was going on and figure out a way to never go through it again.

I could step back and ask myself why it happened and have a plan moving forward to not get myself into the avoidable stuff ever again.

I am realistic enough to know I can't avoid it all. I can't avoid the death of a loved one. I can't control the economy. I could, however, choose to take better care of my own health. I could choose to set money aside in case the economy shifted, which it periodically does. I could choose to learn and continually move forward moving on from the shit happening around me.

Shit will continue to happen. What you plan to do about it when it does happen is the key.

Rule #5)
Patience is Bullshit

"Everybody says that life takes patience, but nobody wants to wait."
Nickelback, from the song After the Rain

I WANT EVERYONE TO PRAY. I really believe in the power of prayer. I don't want you to pray for patience. I believe we have a God with a sense of humor. He will grant you patience, which isn't what you want.

You see, patience is bullshit! Who wants patience? Who said we wanted to wait for our day, our moment or our time?

No one!

It is easy to get sucked into the world's view of how things should be done. It is easy to get lost in the opinions of others.

You will hear all of these bullshit so-called logical phrases:

Just wait your turn.

Your time will come.

Bide your time.

All of those things are bullshit. Forget the small-thinking mentality of this world.

Have you ever heard someone pray for patience? I am such a strong believer in the power of prayer that I think that is the last thing one should pray for.

What if, instead of praying for patience, you prayed for strength? What if you prayed for perseverance? What if you prayed for willpower? What if you simply gave thanks for whatever obstacle lies in your path?

> *"Therefore, since we have been justified through faith, we have peace with God our Lord Jesus Christ, through whom we have gained access by faith into this grace in which we now stand. And we boast in the hope of the glory of God. Not only so, we also glory in our sufferings, because we know that suffering produces perseverance; perseverance, character; and character, hope. And hope does not put us to shame, because God's love has been poured out into our hearts through the Holy Spirit, who has been given to us."*
>
> *Romans 5:1-5*

Why would you possibly give thanks for an obstacle? It is simple. Overcoming that obstacle has the power to lead you to the breakthroughs you are seeking in your life!

> *"Blessed is the one who perseveres under trial because, having stood the test, that person will receive a crown of life that the Lord has promised to those who love him."*
>
> *James 1:12*

When I started in real estate, I was told that I needed to be patient. The success I wanted would take time, maybe years to achieve.

I had a lot of problems with this advice. The biggest one was that I couldn't afford to have it take time. I literally had no time for patience. I needed to pound the phones, hold Open Houses, secure new clients, and close deals.

I had bills to pay! You know, when you have kids, they want to eat. When you have a family, they want to feel secure and that takes money, not patience.

It takes a lot of perseverance to get through the dark days.

If I had asked my family for patience, it probably would have gone something like this:

"Hey, Melissa?"

"Yeah?"

"Well, as you know, I am taking this new career path."

"Yeah. I noticed you stopped going to the other job."

"Yeah. It was time for a change and I need you to trust me that it will all be for the better."

"I trust you. I'm sure it will work out fine. It always does."

"Thanks. I appreciate that."

"No problem. Was there something else? You have this look that seems to be telling me you have something else to say."

"Well, there is one more thing I need from you and the kids."

"Yeah? What is it?"

"Well, I need you all to be patient."

"What do you mean, be patient?"

"Well...I may not make any money for a while."

"How long is a while?"

"I have been talking to some people that told me it could take a while to make any money at all. It could be months or even a year. They said, I will need to be patient. I need to let this progress. I will eventually either make money or fall on my face."

"You are kidding, right?"

"No. We may need to eat ramen for a while. It will all be worth it though. You just have to be patient."

"That isn't going to work."

She would have been right. It wouldn't have worked. Patience doesn't pay the bills. Patience doesn't make dreams come true. Patience is for wishful thinkers. It is for those that believe if they just wait and play by the rules, things will work out.

But the rules of mediocrity are not for you.

None of these rules will talk about living a mediocre life. God didn't make you to be mediocre. He made you to win. Why would he make people in His image to be less than capable of greatness? That logic doesn't work. It only makes sense if you give in to the general outlook of society.

Go to school. Get a job. Don't make any waves. Retire with a pension and live happily ever after.

That is all bullshit and shortsighted thinking. That is all living a patient life, a conformist life.

So, how does one overcome patience?

First, don't ask for it or receive it. You need to simply refuse it.

Second, you have to grind instead.

Grinding is when you work towards a goal in a focused "Don't give a shit what the world throws at you" way.

I am not going to lie. This will take some mental strength. The world seems to enjoy throwing obstacles in your path that can dissuade you from achieving greatness. I will get more in depth on the grind in "Success and Failure Both Leave Clues" rule.

Let me explain what *isn't* patience.

Starting a new job at the bottom isn't patience if certain things are taken into account. Are you trying to learn everything about a company to someday run that business or a similar one? That would make perfect sense. That is a strong use of patience knowing you have levels of knowledge to gain before you can move upwards.

Let's be real though. Don't take me as being okay with this as patience in a laid back sort of way. I want you to learn what needs to be learned as fast as possible and advance in your endeavor.

God talks about periods of waiting that occur in our lives. That makes sense when you bring a little logic to it. You don't start in the mailroom on a Monday and end up being president of Wocka Wocka Wocka Industries that Friday. No, you will have periods of waiting in there where you will be learning the company, learning the craft, and learning how to lead as you advance positions.

I once worked at a music store. I thought I wanted to own a record store. What is the best way to learn how to run a music store? Work at one, of course. I put the time in and learned everything from how to interact with customers, how supply and distribution played into the right or wrong inventory stock, overhead of all kinds and the hours and sales needed to be successful. So, what was the biggest thing that I learned? I learned that I didn't want to own a record store! That was a huge learning lesson.

That wasn't a story in patience. That was a story in gaining knowledge to see if it was the path to success I wanted to take. Turns out, I saved myself from what would have been a bad decision for me. Maybe not a bad decision for others, but definitely in my eyes.

Now, let's look at real estate. There is a lot to learn. You have to know contracts inside and out, inventory, market analysis, communication skills, buyer and seller psychology, etc. That is why I was told I needed to be patient. You know now my feeling on patience. It is complete bullshit.

How did I get around the patience excuse of others? I decided that I would fail forward fast. I would make mistakes and make them quickly. If I made mistakes, I could cut the learning curve down and make money. I may even make money along the way.

So, I did just that. I took every appointment I could get. I signed any listing that would let me put a sign in the yard. I met with every potential buyer possible whether I knew if they were qualified to buy yet or not. I studied *successful* agents. I watched training videos, practiced scripts and how to overcome objections. I did all of this to shorten a learning curve down to as small of a time frame as possible.

On top of all of that, I got myself a coach, a mentor, who had been there and achieved a level of success where I wanted to be. We role-played what happened going into and out of these appointments. By continually fine-tuning through the lessons learned, I got better and better at my career in a significantly shorter amount of time.

I decided to accept the fact that I could learn as I went and shorten my period of waiting. I was okay with learning, but I wasn't going to sit back and be patient that success would come without applying action to it. I worked long hours. I sacrificed a lot of meaningless activities like watching TV to make the learning curve, the time I was supposed to be patient, shorter.

You see, exercising patience in all of this would have been the completely wrong approach with bullshit results. I would have more than likely been just another statistic.

In real estate, the failure rate for first year agents is right around 97%. Of the remaining 3%, 90% of them will be out of real estate after their second year. Why is that?

They are broke. Not only financially, but physically and mentally, too.

So, if that is the end result, what was the cause?

My feeling is that they were patient. They bought into the stories that the agents they knew had told them. They believed when people said to them, they would be lucky to sell one or two homes their first year and locked into that line of thinking. They may have thought that if people knew they were in real estate, they would just get business. They would fall into an investor or fix and flipper that would give them mountains of money to play with. They would live the TV life. Hell, they may even get their own reality show!

What if instead of being patient and waiting for things to happen, they had instead made things happen? Good things *may* come to those who wait, but they are more likely to happen with action. Why take the chance? Why rely on luck when action has a much better chance of achieving success?

I just need to be patient. My time will come. No way I can get passed over.

That is all bullshit.

Let's look at another example:

If you were to end up in a job that stalls out because the position you want requires someone to retire or die in order to advance, you have some serious thinking to do.

What if instead of being patient in that situation, you made your own fortune? What if you found a way in the company to create a growth opportunity that called for an additional position or one even better because of your ideas? What if your idea propelled the company in such a way that you couldn't be ignored?

Or, if that doesn't work, what if you went out and made a whole new company? Think of the impact you could have on others by not being patient when it comes to success or chasing a dream or goal.

Being patient wouldn't allow any of this. It would say to wait your turn. That is of no benefit to you, your employer, or your family. It is thinking small and accepting the norm.

Did you know that only 61 companies that were in the top 500 companies in 1955 were in the top 500 in 2015? It was in an article published by Mark J. Perry on October 12, 2015 (www.aei.org). He shows a list of those in the top 500 in 1955 and then in 2015. What I saw out of the 61 still around is that they continued to innovate and grow. They didn't rest. They didn't get patient and wait on a market to improve. They pushed forward.

Take a look at these companies and tell me what the failures all had in common.

Here is an excerpt from Mark's article:

> **Group A:** American Motors, Brown Shoe, Studebaker, Collins Radio, Detroit Steel, Zenith Electronics, and National Sugar Refining.

> **Group B:** Boeing, Campbell Soup, General Motors, Kellogg, Proctor and Gamble, John Deere, IBM and Whirlpool.
>
> **Group C:** Facebook, eBay, Home Depot, Microsoft, Google, Netflix, Office Depot and Target.
>
> All of the companies in **Group A** were in the Fortune 500 in 1955, but not in 2015.
>
> All of the companies in **Group B** were in the Fortune 500 in both 1955 and 2015.
>
> All of the companies in **Group C** were in the Fortune 500 in 2015, but not 1955.

I found this completely fascinating.

In Group A, it shows some once great companies that stopped innovating. I believe they needed some impatient innovators. You look at a company like American Motors and it had to be completely absorbed by another company, Chrysler. Zenith fell due to innovators like Vizio.

Group B shows companies that continued to evolve and maintain their foothold in the top 500 companies. Companies such as Kellogg's have continually understood that you must market and push yourself to maintain your foothold. They don't accept that people know who they are. They are impatiently looking for another customer or another way to make a Pop Tart.

General Motors has to keep improving on last year's cars and trucks or end up like Studebaker. They can't point to the 1988 Impala and act like it was good then with it's standard vinyl seats, AM radio and four radial tires so what else do you want or need? Quit your bitching and give me your money!

Group C is interesting. Those are innovators. Seeing how things worked and saying, "Screw that! I have a better idea!" Go back a generation and we had no Facebook. You had no easy way of staying in touch with a lot of people. How else would I know, that Dave is a professor now, or that cute couple in high school is still married 25+ years later?

Netflix has brought portability to your entertainment options. No longer are you tied to the cable or satellite. I can watch Fuller House on my iPad! How cool is that?

Google has made it so easy to know or find anything in a few simple keystrokes. Not only that, but I can buy a domain through them, blog, and store my photos online.

I would bet that, what all companies in Group C have in common, is that they employ people that believe patience is bullshit. They were of action, not of waiting.

Take action. Don't wait. Don't be patient.

Patience is bullshit. It is weak if it doesn't come with some action. Don't sit around waiting for a better day saying your time will come. Get up and make it happen!

Remember that tomorrow is never guaranteed. Patience delays success and failure.

Wait...why do I want failure?

We cover that in the next rule: Success and Failure Both Leave Clues.

RULE #6)
SUCCESS AND FAILURE
BOTH LEAVE CLUES

"Success leaves clues. Be a better observer of the winners and the losers, those who are doing well and those who are falling behind. Take mental notes and say, "I'm going to adjust what I'm doing based on what I see."
– Jim Rohn

I LOVE JIM ROHN AND always felt this quote could be broken down into rule #6. The quote I heard for years was that success leaves clues. I never felt that was the whole story. It missed the point by stopping short of Jim's whole meaning. In fact, I felt it was a half-truth at best. What good is half a lesson?

The reality is, that Success *and* Failure both leave clues. Jim Rohn says as much in the above quote, but so many miss the rest of his point.

Years ago, I came up with rule #6. I hadn't heard the one from Jim Rohn yet. I hadn't started assigning my rules any numbers yet, but I said it all the time. I believed that I could learn more from my failures than from my successes. I was pretty excited when I ran across the whole quote from Jim Rohn. Like I said, many stop after the first sentence.

Michael Jordan won 6 championships with the Chicago Bulls. That is success. I still remember the move he made against the Utah Jazz to hit the game winner. I remember his pass to John Paxton for the game-winning bucket against the Phoenix Suns.I remember all those years during the regular season when they needed a winning basket at the end of the game. They looked to MJ to make it happen. He didn't always make it but you always felt he would. He was the embodiment of a successful basketball player.

Was Michael a gifted athlete and did everything fall in line because of his gift? Where are the failures?

This is taken from a *Newsweek* article Titled, "Michael Jordan Didn't Make Varsity -- At First," on October 17th, 2015.

> *In 1978, Michael Jordan was just another kid in the gym, along with 50 or so of his classmates, trying out for the Emsley A. Laney High School varsity basketball team. There were 15 roster spots. Jordan, then a 15-year-old sophomore who was only 5'10" and could not yet dunk a basketball, did not get one. His close friend, 6'7" sophomore Leroy*

Smith, did. The team was in need of his length. "It was embarrassing not making the team," Jordan later said. He went home, locked himself in his room and cried. He didn't quit there. He picked himself up and turned the cut into motivation.

"Whenever I was working out and got tired and figured I ought to stop, I'd close my eyes and see that list in the locker room without my name on it," Jordan would explain. "That usually got me going again."

Michael didn't start out great. He had to work at it. He took the failures and determined where he needed to make improvements, so eventually and arguably, became the greatest basketball player of all time.

Everyone starts from not knowing enough about a project, or a sport they love, or how to play guitar. We all start from zero. Even if our pedigree says we should know everything there is to know, we don't. We have to learn how to be great at anything and that takes practice.

One of the more frustrating things to grasp in life, when wanting to do something, is that we, well, have to learn it first. I know, that sounds so simple.

"Duh! Of course I have to learn it before I know it!"

Yeah, if only our brains worked with such simple logic all the time.

"Don't go through life, grow through life."
Eric Butterworth

I love music. I have this crazy knowledge of bands deep into the melodic rock world. It goes way beyond the bands that everyone knows. The thing is, I didn't start with all that knowledge. I had to learn it.

I am successful in my goofy music knowledge because I learned it.

As you learn anything in life, you will have failure. You will have setbacks.

When I started in real estate, I knew nothing about it. I knew I could be good at it if I put the work in, but I had little knowledge yet to back up this claim. I would show up in the office every morning at 7:30am and leave around 10pm. I studied contracts, scripts for phone calls, watched training videos from successful agents, watched market update videos as well as live training several days a week. I read anything about real estate. I studied the psychology of buyers and sellers. I took every appointment I could, knowing I would screw up a lot of them, because I was learning.

I had to fail many times. I had no choice. I had to write offers and not get them accepted. I had to lose clients because I said the wrong thing. I had to watch the potential client walk away because I said the wrong thing. I had to go to my business coach many times with tail between my legs and apologize for being so dumb when it came to working with humans.

I had to learn to accept a lot of *No, Nope,* and *Never.*

I had a choice to make. I could learn from these failures or I could quit.

Failure is only permanent if you stop trying to be successful.

The real estate industry has some of the highest failure rates of any occupation. Around 97% of agents quit after a year. They can't handle the *No's*, so they just give up.

They quit. They blamed everyone but themselves for their failures.

It can't possibly be their fault. They didn't learn from their failures.

I knew the odds when I got in. Everyone told them to me. They said I would starve. They told me that you had to know people to be successful and even that was no guarantee.

In spite of the odds, I didn't care. I almost took it as a challenge.

It reminds me of the line in *Dumb and Dumber*. Jim Carrey's character, Lloyd, asked Mary if she would date him.

Lloyd "The least you can do is level with me. What are my chances?"

Mary "Not good."

Lloyd "You mean, not good like one out of a hundred?"

Mary "I'd say more like one out of million."

Lloyd "So, you are telling me there's a chance? YEAH!"

I only had 3% odds to make it a year? Cool. Let's do this. Odds have never scared me so why should I let that number bother me?

What did I know that others needed to know?

Those odds pertained to others. They didn't define me. I didn't have to follow them. I didn't have to conform. Failures or successes were up to me. Which average did I want to be, 97% or 3%?

The funny thing about statistics is that they are just that. They are numbers. One can be the example of those stats or the exception. Being the exception is where success is built.

You only join the 97% when you make the current failure your last one. It is okay to fail as long as it is progressing you towards success.

Fail forward.

Each time you fail, you need to learn from it.

In Matthew Syed's book, *Black Box Thinking*, he tells a story about Unilever. They were having problems with a nozzle. They were inefficient, kept getting clogged, and made detergent grains of different sizes.

Matthew tells how, out of desperation, they turned to their biologist to fix the problem. They had a profound understanding of the relationship between failure and success. They took ten copies of the nozzles and applied small changes to them. They would take the best of the ten. Maybe it only improved things by one or two percent. This nozzle would then be varied, with the improvement, another ten times. After 45 generations and 449 failures, they had a nozzle that was outstanding.

Take your failures, make a minor adjustment and move forward with the improved plan. Your goal with failure isn't instant improvement, but one of degrees.

I still find myself making adjustments off of flaws, failures and shortcomings in my life and business to this day. The fun thing is, I don't ever see this ever stopping. Such is the beauty of life and the continual strive for success in business or just being a better human.

I don't believe everlasting success is possible without failure along the way. We learn so much more from failure than we ever learn from success. With success, we see an end product. In the failure, if it is improved on, we see the true story of success.

Success is the what. It shows an end result. It is the climax of the struggle. We need to know the failure prior to that first.

Failing forward is the "Why."

The Chicago Cubs won the World Series in 2016 ending a drought of 108 years between baseball championships. They achieved the pinnacle of success in their sport and could shed the "Lovable Losers" moniker. I can't imagine that any of them wanted to be looked at as losers, even lovable ones.

So, where did the changes start? When did they make a shift in culture to be winners and not losers? When did they decide to start failing forward rather than just fail?

This brings me to the year 2009. Yep, it all started in 2009. For decades, the Tribune Company owned the Chicago Cubs. In 2009, Thomas Ricketts became the majority owner of the Cubs. They had the first piece of the puzzle, a fan of the team, in control. Following this, the Cubs went to work rebuilding a depleted minor league system, growing talent from within.

In November of 2014, they brought in Joe Madden to be the next coach, signing him to a five-year contract. Joe had already shown his managerial gift by leading the Tampa Bay Rays to multiple winning seasons with little budget to work with. The fans, rightly so, were excited to see what he could do with a budget to acquire the missing pieces needed to win it all--something Tampa Bay simply couldn't afford to do.

In 2015, they came close. They made it all the way to the National League Championship, but were swept by the New York Mets. They had a choice to make at the end of that year. Learn from the failure and move forward or repeat the recipe of prior years when this failure set the whole franchise back.

They chose to learn. This failure showed they needed to add a few pieces and let a couple go. They didn't need to scrap all of it, but add in a few players and they could win. They brought in Ben Zobrist, Jason Heyward and Jon Lackey.

In 2016, the Cubs won 103 games. This was the first time they won over 100 games since 1935. They went on to beat the Giants and Dodgers to make the World Series for the first time since 1945. Coming from a three games to one deficit, they went on to beat the Cleveland Indians in the World Series. Ben Zobrist, one of the players added in the off-season, went on to win the World Series MVP.

Fail, fail a lot, and fail as much as possible.

But, make sure it is failure that is moving you forward towards success.

Don't just fail for failures sake.

Everything I have said is pointless unless you take that failure and learn, and take ownership and accept it.

What did you do wrong? Hey, if you didn't get the sale, you did something wrong. You can blame the other party, but it is on you. So what was the reason?

Did you talk too much? It is possible to lose the sale after you won the sale. You let your sales guard down and inserted the foot in the mouth or you named a feature that it doesn't or can't have with it.

Did you talk too little? Scripts are essential in sales. At least have something basic memorized or in a presentation that keeps the conversation going.

Did you not answer all their questions? If they aren't asking questions, it isn't their fault. You are the one selling them on what you have to offer. This applies whether you are looking to sell something, make a friend, or ask a girl out on a date. You have to win that person over to you. If you answer someone's questions, they get to know you and what you have to offer. If they aren't asking questions, you need to be doing that. You need to make the conversation flow.

Were you late? A lot of people, myself included, loathe when people are late. Yes. I *loathe* when people are late. Most, like myself, view it as disrespectful. To come back from that is near impossible. Learn your lesson and show up on time, or better yet, early, the next time you have an appointment. You may be able to apologize to them and win it back but that is not always the case. Again, this is not just in business, but also in your personal life.

How did you dress? In sales, you need to dress to impress. Don't show up in blue jeans and a t-shirt to a multi million dollar deal until you are the go-to baller and everybody wants a piece of you. Even then, I would still go with a touch of class.

Did you come across as greedy or selfish? Look, we all know that in sales you are there to make money. Awesome! Just remember that the other person wants to know you care before they give you a dime of their money.

Did you show confidence? Coming across as less than confident is a great way to shut down a date or kill a business deal every time. I have done some of my best business deals when I have had no money in the bank. I squished down the greed and neediness I was feeling and sold my confidence that I could get the deal done.

Did you tell any stories? Man, I love stories. When I need to drive a point home, I love to tell a story that relates to their situation. If you don't have your own stories, pick the brains of other successful people in your industry. I have had clients repeat my own stories back to me when I needed a price reduction. They won't remember the comparable homes sold prices based on XYZ features but they will remember a good story. I have collected a lot of them and tell them over and over again.

How did you leave it? If you failed to get the sale, did you set yourself up for the follow up and a chance down the line? Never close the door entirely. Give yourself a chance to come back again if the timing isn't right.

Did you try multiple times to get the sale? You need to ask them multiple times to do business with you. You may not get a second chance. You need to know you gave your all when they were in front of you.

Could you have tried something differently? Hey, even in the dating world, if you find that your pickup line to get a pretty girl or cute guy to talk to you isn't working, are you going to keep using it? In sales, if you have a bad pitch that gets low results, why are you not changing it?

Those are just a handful of questions you should be asking yourself.

Never take the failure at face value. That does nothing to help you improve. Figure out what you could do to improve and you will bounce back, and be on a path to success, much faster.

Success leaves clues. So does failure. The money, the true success, will come from the failures.

RULE #7)
SAY THANK YOU

"Give thanks in all circumstances, for this
is God's will in you through Christ Jesus."
1 Thessalonians 5:18 NIV

THIS COULD BE A TOUGH one. Definitely, hard when times are tough. Why would you ever want to be thankful during those times?

So, let's start with the easy "thank you" first.

I have made it a point, whether I am getting an energy drink at the local QuikTrip, or paying for my pumpkin protein shake at Jamba Juice, that I will look the clerk in the eyes and say thank you.

Better yet, I make sure I mean it.

This is something simple. Start here.

Next, let's level this up.

Have you watched the world around you lately? I mean, have you really watched it? I am not talking about online through Facebook, Twitter or Instagram. I mean the real world.

I challenge you to go out without your cell phone. I know, it is a scary thought being disconnected from all the likes, hearts and thumbs up of social media, but trust me. Give it a try and take a look at what is going on outside.

Do me a favor and go participate in the greatest of all social platforms and people watch. Take a look around our world. You will see we have become a world more obsessed with the electronic screen in front of our face, and the opinions of people that we don't really know, than the people in it.

I want you to be different and adult better.

When you pass someone, say hello or give a nod and a smile. It may take a little practice but your smile will develop a wondrous genuine feel and shake off the creepy stalker vibe.

For some, it will take longer than others.

Strike up a conversation with people. Hey, it will initially startle people! It will also be uncomfortable. So what? If you are coming from a place of love, most humans will see it. Get to know your fellow humans on a personal interactive level.

Then, thank them for talking to you, or wish them a great rest of their day.

Life is tough. You could be the light that gets someone through the day.

I purposely go out, most of the time, in a concert t-shirt or a fun shirt, like Mario or super heroes.

My wife and I were at Costco last month, and my Iron Maiden shirt led to 3 meaningful conversations. To some, that would drive them mad. They are in a hurry going from stop to stop in a race to get back home.

To me, it led to an opportunity to human better.

I truly believe we are starving. Not for food, but for real attention. We are starving for people to not only notice us but to care.

These interactions are simple if you just slow down and notice each other. These are the easy ways to say, "Thank you" or bless someone else's day.

Thank God for the beauty of this world.

Now, what about when times are tough or a situation clearly shows that in that moment there is nothing, seemingly, to be thankful for?

I understand that. In the moment, the pain may not be to your benefit though. It may be a moment you have to go through that is unexplainable and unfair right now. Its purpose could be years in the making. It could be necessary for you to go through it now, and to survive it, in order for you to help someone else later on. You may need to survive to help someone else.

Although, it will be hard to be thankful for the pain you suffer, you will be thankful that you were able to help someone else get through it.

My parents divorced when I was 2. Why should I be thankful they ever did that? Moving forward, I got them each part time. We rotated holidays. Summers in Iowa instead of at home in

Illinois with my friends from school. Then, the unthinkable happens. They remarry.

I can look back now and see plenty of reasons to be thankful. Yeah, my parents divorced and that sucked, but, what I gained was incredible and something to truly be thankful for.

Some of the important things that I gained were four more brothers and a sister. When I went to my Dad's house in Iowa, we had enough for a basketball team or half a baseball team. If we gathered a few more neighborhood kids, we had a game! It was never boring and I am forever blessed for those memories.

I learned life lessons from my new siblings as well as my extra parents. I learned how to properly change a tire, and do basic maintenance on a car, from my stepfather. I also saw what it means to man up when my mother got ill. I will never forget the compassion he showed her before she died.

One of the people I am most thankful for is my stepsister, Cheryl. I learned how to be strong in my faith from her. If not for my parents divorcing and remarrying, I never would have known her.

It wasn't all sunshine and rainbows. I didn't always see eye to eye with my new parents. I would be lying if I said I was always thankful for our situation, but I can look back now and say it has made me more understanding and compassionate to others living a blended family life style. I have a relatable story to show them that it doesn't have to be a bad thing.

You want to know what else was awesome about growing up in a blended family? We had multiple Christmas parties to go to!

Hello! More presents!

My parents got divorced (Boo!!!), but we had more Christmas parties (Yay!!!).

I don't believe we are ever given more than we can handle. Our God knows what we are capable of handling. We are pretty resilient humans.

In the moment, it may have felt like life was unfair. I know that when I lost a job, I felt it wasn't fair. How could they not see my awesomeness? How could they not see the value I brought?

Going through the tough times have made me stronger. I learned so much from every difficult time. These lessons were carried forward. I find myself pulling from those moments every day.

Let's look at losing a job. Why should I have been thankful?

Well, it opened my eyes to other opportunities. It made me realize that there were other jobs. As crazy as that sounds, I have found that I can get so bogged down in the repetition of the day in and day out routine of work, I can lose sight of all the world has to offer. By exiting a job, either by choice or not, I have been able to refocus on what matters most as far as my goals in life are concerned.

I was drowning in the quicksand of mediocrity and had no clue!

My eyes were opened because I went through the bad times.

When bad times happen, which they will, take a step back and try something counterintuitive.

Instead of saying "Why me? Try and say, "Why not me?"

I know. That sounds ridiculous. If you lose a job or a loved one, the pain is tremendous. It makes little sense to just accept it.

Acceptance is an important step towards being thankful in all situations.

Don't forget, God knows what you can handle. He has a plan. He isn't going to give you more than you can handle. So, if it seems like you are at a point where life is giving you nothing to be thankful for, or that all it offers is pain and misery, understand one thing:

God thinks you are a bad ass.

Out of every good time or hard time in your life, give thanks. Just say, "Thank You."

Rule #8)
Live Epic

"Life is way too short to live a crappy life."
– Kevin Belzer

I HAVE HAD SOMEWHERE AROUND 33 jobs. My children think this is hilarious. Truthfully, until I was 36, I didn't find much point in sticking around at jobs or career paths that didn't motivate me anymore. Once I got the value I wanted out of them, I moved on. It took me until the last few years to really analyze and figure out why I was like this.

Growing up as a child in the greatest decade, the '80s, I was bombarded with some great movies. Some of the greats were *The Breakfast Club, Pretty in Pink, Fast Times at Ridgemont High, Raiders of the Lost Ark, Sixteen Candles...* well, the list goes on. They all had this common thread running through them. Everyone was overcoming something or finding where they belonged. Since my brain was this growing pile of mush, It was influenced heavily by these movies.

I have always desired to live a life of purpose. I have strived to push myself to be better, to experience more, and to overcome all that life throws at me. I thank the '80s for this drive.

So, what is an epic life?

Why are you here? Why were you born? What were you meant to do? What is your purpose?

In moments of quiet reflection, I expect some or all of these questions to consume your thoughts. For me, they have continually done this.

At times, I have questioned life and my purpose. I have wondered whether I have gotten everything out of what I have been offered. The biggest thing offered has been time.

Time is something that can't be bought or bartered for. Once it is gone, passed by, or neglected and taken for granted, it doesn't return. You get no second chance to enjoy the time you lost or wasted.

Do you waste your time watching TV or being distracted by what others are doing while you do nothing? Hey, I have. I am not perfect. I have moments where that is all I want to do.

On occasion, I have to remind myself that life can be and should be, so much more than binge-watching Breaking Bad or playing video games. I don't believe these things are necessarily wrong activities, but I do believe they should be monitored. They should not be what life was all about. I don't see any of us on our deathbed wishing we had watched one more hour of

TV, played one more hour of video games, or watched one more hour of cat videos.

I think what we will be doing is wishing we had more meaningful time to reflect back. What if you had gone and knocked another item off of your bucket list instead of spending some weekend on the couch binge-watching season 3 of *Orange Is the New Black?*

As I mentioned, I have been at 33 different jobs. I don't say this to brag. It took me a while to realize what I wanted to roll out of bed for everyday and call a career. Although I am happy in what I do, I also know that my life goals are continually changing, and in ten years, I may be off doing something else.

That is okay.

In an epic life, one should never feel that they have to be stuck in whatever moment they are in forever. You should always look at things as being able to be improved upon or replaced. You should be continually growing and adding to your experiences.

Last year, we took a vacation for 2 weeks to New York City and Bermuda. We explored and saw all the cool sites we had on our bucket list like the Empire State Building, Time Square, Grand Central Station and the World Trade Center Memorial. A favorite photo is of our family on top of the Empire State Building. The backdrop is of the nighttime city skyline. I look at that photo and smile every time. Let's not forget us indulging in a different pizza place everyday. We truly fell in love with New York, walking and exploring it from morning until night.

We took a cruise to Bermuda and were able to just relax and have great conversations, see comedy shows, and eat whenever we wanted. Walking on the deck and having time with the family that was uninterrupted, by the normal nonstop ringing of my phone, was wonderful.

Upon arriving in Bermuda, we went to the pink sand beaches and swam in the cove. We explored the island and got that taste of island life that is addictive. We went on a night glass-bottomed boat tour of the Bermuda Triangle. My son and I went kayaking there as well. To see the joy on a 14-year-old kids face is priceless.

My takeaway from that trip was simple: Live epically.

You may be independently wealthy, able to drop it all at a moment's notice and live epically all the time. For me, and most humans, work must occur for the money to be exchanged to then hopefully enjoy some of the epic experiences that life has to offer.

My priorities at 36 years of age changed. Rather than work a lot to make a lot of money, I wanted to find a way to work less for the same money. From the ages of 33-36, I worked two full time jobs. I made what I thought was good money at the time, but worked six days a week from 7:30am until midnight.

I had a friend tell me about a real estate opportunity. If he hadn't said something, I doubt I would have changed anything I was doing. I was so tired and was in a rut. I didn't know this though. I was too tired and into my work to see what I was doing.

I was living but had no life.

What I saw was an opportunity to take my life back. I knew I would have to initially "pay my dues", but then I could eventually have the time and money to do all the things I wanted to do.

I looked at a career change as my opportunity to shift into a different life more aligned to my long-term goals and dreams. I saw it as an opportunity to use the income it produced to start checking off the items on my bucket list.

I suggest making a bucket list. A bucket list is a list of things you want to do in your life before you die. That may seem morbid, but let's get real. We are all going to die eventually.

The real question is whether you actually lived.

Look at a bucket list as a list of goals. It could have skydiving, whitewater rafting, singing at a karaoke bar or trying root beer milk or even have $1 million in the bank. It is your list, so you can put whatever you want on it. Do you want to go on a cruise? That was on mine. Go to the top of the Empire State building? That was on mine as well. It can have anything you want it to have on it.

It can be simple to extreme. Mine has encompassed a mix of both.

An example of a simple item on my list was that I wanted to coach my son, "Bubba", in little league. Pretty simple on the surface but it required me taking a hard look at what my priorities were in life. I could see that changes had to be made to make this happen. I felt it was important for myself as a father and memories for my son to make this a priority on my bucket list. I have now coached my son for five years.

I believe life is best lived when it has purpose and goals around it. A bucket list is a simple way to put those goals in front of you.

As our trip last summer started feeling more like a reality and less like a dream, I got more excited. I thought about all I wanted to knock off the bucket list. I would go on the cruise website and check out shore excursions. I always wanted to kayak and that was an option! We could take a boat excursion to the Bermuda Triangle? Sweet! I always wanted to go to the Bermuda Triangle!

Do yourself a favor. Write your bucket list down. Set a timeframe of when you will do them. Don't say someday. Living epic requires action.

Living epic can bleed over into your work. To pay for all you want to do can lead to an increase in productivity at your job.

It definitely gave me more motivation in my work life to make sure I could do all these things.

It is twofold. One, you are motivated by the money. The money is necessary to pay for travel, skydiving, kayaking and even trying root beer milk. Two, you will find your production increase. Driven to succeed outside of a job in the world can't help but bleed over into your work. Happy, motivated, driven people perform better and have more value at their job or occupation. You may find the exception to this, but how many people who spend their free time binge watching Netflix are also the most innovating top producing humans at a company?

Motivated goal-driven people live longer, not necessarily in years on the planet, but in meaningful hours on this planet. You could live to be 100 years old, but never actually live. You could, however, live to 45 and leave behind a legacy that makes people go "Wow, that human lived!"

Don't misread that. I am not advocating that dying young is awesome. That isn't my point. The point I am making is that just because you lived long, it doesn't mean it had any purpose or that you lived an epic life. You could have spent all those years watching General Hospital, smoking cigarettes and eating bonbons. That isn't exactly epic or inspiring.

I can't really give you an example of someone who lived long that made no impact. Because they left no impact, they are unknown. Let me give you an example, though, of someone who did live epically. I was sad when this person died, but I remember thinking about all he did and what he left behind. That was what inspired me.

On August 4th, 2006, Steve Irwin died at the age of 44. He was best known as the Crocodile Hunter. He had a show on TV that documented him and his wife's life. He was the owner of an Australian Zoo. His mission was to educate people on the nature world and all it's wonderful animals. The viewership of his show reached millions of people around the world! Over the course of the show, we saw the zoo expand. Steve Irwin had a platform to champion environmental causes to protect the habitats of the animals that he showed every week on his show and specials. He was a guest star on *The Tonight Show with Jay Leno*. He was involved in countless foundations and animal rehab and rescue facilities.

We see today his family carry on his legacy by continuing to run the zoo and educate people on our wondrous animal kingdom. I recently saw one of them on Jimmy Fallon and educating people on a few animals that were brought on the program. The Australian government even set aside 334k acres for a national park naming it Steve Irwin Wildlife Reserve.

By living epically, others were impacted in a positive way by Steve Irwin.

You can inspire others by what you do as well. Living epically not only benefits you, but the world. We humans are motivated, excited, or directed, for better or worse, by those around us.

Why not impact humanity for the better?

If you see someone else set a goal to run a marathon, you may initially sit back and watch what happens next. You see them start training for it. You see them push through the pain and keep going. Maybe they start looking fit. They start carrying themselves differently. They seem to have more confidence. The day of the race comes and they do it! They run a marathon.

You start to think and wonder if you can do that. You wonder what it would feel like to run a marathon. That person seems so different. Maybe you want to feel different too. They seem better...like they accomplished something huge.

Will it change me as well?

You now have the itch to try something epic as well. It is something scary to you because it is new, but that is okay. You want to feel what they feel. You *need* to feel what they feel.

I believe that you should live epically, not just for you, for those around you. The impact you can have on the world can carry on past the time you die. Steve Irwin lived an epic life. I didn't even highlight everything he did and it seems like a daunting amount.

Let's start asking ourselves a different series of questions.

What if you were epic every opportunity you got?

If you always strive to live life to the fullest, what would be different? In your job, would your employer look at you differently? I bet they would. Go-getters get attention. If they appreciate it, you will move up in your company and take on more responsibility with more reward (money and recognition) attached to it. If they don't appreciate it, take that as a sign to move along to a company that does appreciate your talents and drive.

How about the self-employed? Would your clients look at you differently? Would they value you more? I bet they would refer others to you as well. Why wouldn't they? Humans like to work with and refer to other humans that they trust. If they think you are barely getting the job done, they may tolerate you for that transaction but they won't be referring you.

Only the epic will get consistent recognition for a job well done.

What would be better in my life?

Better yet, what wouldn't? Have you ever had a feeling of a void in your life? It is that longing in your soul screaming out that there must be more to this life.

Guess what? There is more to this life. If you consistently live an epic life, there is no room for a void.

Satisfaction comes from living an epic life.

David Cassidy, the singer and star of the Partridge Family, passed away in 2017. His last words were, "So much wasted time."

Are you wasting your time? Do you want to look back on the years and think it was wasted time or do you want to look back at it differently?

So, what would be better in your life? Everything. It would all be better. How could it not be?

What change can you bring to the world?

Change comes in many different ways. It can bring national change like Martin Luther King did. He has impacted generations beyond his time on earth. For having a short life, he lived epically big time.

It can be local change like helping at a food bank or fostering kids. These may not seem epic on the surface but they inspire and help others. Besides, what is not epic about feeding the hungry or helping a child through whatever difficulties his parents are dealing with? Your help could be what inspires those people, or that child, to live for better and more epic things through the years ahead.

What examples can you set for people?

Give everything you've got at a job or career. You are setting an example for others of what hard work can accomplish.

Whether you train for a marathon, write a song, or sky dive, you can inspire someone. If you overcome difficulties that life throws at you and become successful, you went epic by inspiring someone else. Then, others see that it is possible to win no matter what life throws your way.

Even if you don't succeed and overcome, but you show strength and the unwillingness to give up, you inspire and give hope. I know it may not seem epic to fail, but a "never quit" and a "never give up" attitude is inspiring. It is epic and it should be celebrated.

Maybe, it wasn't about a particular day or moment, but an attitude you displayed on your epic journey. What if that becomes part of your legacy towards an epic life that you will look back on with pride and a smile?

What is your legacy?

What is it now, and what do you want it to be? Don't be ashamed, or sad, if it isn't where you want it to be. Make the decision to change it! Make the "where you are" inspire someone later on when you arrive, when you overcome, when you become the epic person that God intended you to be.

We all have the opportunity to leave a lasting legacy that will inspire others. The path we all must travel will be different. I believe God does this to show others, to inspire them that you can come from money or poverty, sickness or health and inspire others of what this world has to offer and what living, really living, is all about.

As I write this, I think about my legacy and what I want to

leave for others. What did my life mean, and what did it say about me? I want to know that I didn't waste any of it. I want to know that I showed others a way to be a better human.

So, I leave this rule with one simple question:

How are you going to live your epic life?

RULE #9)
FIND LOVE

As iron sharpens iron, so one
person sharpens another.
-Proverbs 27:17

FROM A YOUNG AGE, I was in search of love. It goes back to handing out Valentine's cards to all the girls in grade school. The struggle is real as you have that first thought of how you sign the card. Do I sign it, "From Kevin" or "Love Kevin"? This was unimaginable pressure on my little brain. In third grade, I am being forced to make a choice. One could very well hold the future to pure bliss and happiness, and 50 years or more of marriage and scores of children.

Or, I could say love to the wrong girl, and she could do the equivalent of burning me in effigy with her public scorn and teasing.

Ahh! What do I do, I thought.

I had a lot of confidence as a third grader. I was everything a girl could want in a long-term mate. At least, that is what I told myself. I decided to make the executive decision that I would do some cards as "from" and others as "love". I just knew that if I said "love" to all of them, I would have to break a lot of hearts. That would not be fair to these wonderful girls. One of them could be my future wife if I played this out perfectly.

I toiled over the cards that night. I decided on the chosen few that would be considered for a future spouse, and delivered them around to the desks at the designated time the following day. I waited.

All day I waited. I was expecting this onslaught of love pouring my way, begging me to pick them as their future spouse. Soon, we would have to arrange for my mom to drive me over to meet their parents. It was best to get on their good side early. We would be getting married as soon as we were through the next 9 grades and out of high school.

The day came and went.

Nothing.

Okay. That's fine. I get that they all had a ton of cards to go through. They would probably read them tonight and seek me out tomorrow.

The next day, I waited. I tried stealing sly looks towards the girls I had narrowed down to, but couldn't get a read. I now started questioning myself.

Had I cast too small of a net? Was my brilliant plan somehow flawed? This seemed ludicrous but it might be possible. Maybe I should have told them all that I loved them.

I didn't give up. This was my dream and it would eventually become my reality. I was sure of it.

I would not give up on love.

* * *

I grew up in a blended family. My parents divorced when I was two years old. Both parents remarried. The new mom and dad both had kids they brought into the family. Almost overnight, I went from having one brother to having three brothers and a sister.

In hindsight, I wouldn't change any of this. I gained more brothers and a sister. Without my parents getting divorced and remarried, I wouldn't have them or the children they made.

That said, from an early age, I had it in my mind that I would never go through a divorce. I would find someone to spend 50 plus years with, God willing. I wanted the forever love and the happily ever after.

I dated sporadically in high school. I had my continual crushes but nothing ever lasted longer than 4 months. I was always in search of "The One".

I can admit now that I was a little cold and calculating in how I looked at this whole dating thing. I was trying to find love. If I didn't think it was going to work, I moved on. I can't say I was the nicest about it, or that it ever made sense to the poor girl whose heart got broken. It probably made no sense to anyone else around, for that matter. Heck, sometimes it made little sense to me as I was making a lot of decisions on instinct or gut. I even tried to justify one of the breakups in some sappy ass letter. Sappy may be putting it a little too nicely. It was immature at best. Ugh...I was pathetic and cold.

After high school, I went to basic training for the Illinois National Guard. When I got back, I needed a job and applied at a Hardee's in Morton, Illinois.

Almost immediately, I started dating a girl there, but it became pretty evident she was still hung up on her last boyfriend. About the time this fell apart, my now wife asked me out.

Well, that is her version.

Here is the true story.

Melissa was very shy. She had her friend Troy sit me down in the lobby with her and Troy across from me. He asked me on a date for her. She invited me to a play at Illinois Central College.

Melissa and I went to the play, and spent every waking hour over the next 10 days together. One night, we were at my dumpy apartment that had no working heat and it was rolling past midnight into December 7th, 1990. I didn't realize the date when I did what I did next. Some of the best things in life are unplanned.

There we were, cuddled together, reading a Calvin and Hobbes book.

Really. I can't make that up.

I said," You know, we should get married."

I just knew. 10 days after we started dating, I knew she was the one with whom I wanted to spend the rest of my life. I couldn't think of a single reason not to ask her to marry me and get on to "happily ever after."

I was smitten. I was head over heels in love.

She shrugs her shoulders and says, "Okay" and keeps reading the comic book.

"I'm serious. We should get married. I mean, we really like each other. Why should we wait?" It was that simple. I found love and wanted to enjoy life with her. I couldn't imagine a life without her in it.

She shrugs her shoulders again, looks at me, smiles, and says, "Okay" again, then back to reading the comic book.

She still didn't believe I wasn't kidding. So, I asked her, "Should I get down on one knee to make it official?" She stopped reading, looked at me for a moment, smiled, and proclaimed, "Okay! Yes!"

I called my brother, Scott, and told him first that I just asked her to marry me. He didn't believe me at first, but happy nonetheless.

* * *

I also can't imagine a world without knowing or sharing love...

Proverbs 27:17 spoke about another sharpening you and

that is what is so great about love. It shows us a side of humanity that is beautiful.

We are not meant to live life alone.

Love can come from your spouse but it can also come elsewhere.

I advice you to have strong friendships, people you care about deeply and that also care for you. God never intended for us to be alone.

If those around you do nothing but criticize and cut you down, they aren't your friends and they don't love you.

One of the saddest things is when people stay in the same circle of "friends" who do nothing but tell others how little they are worth. If you think you can't do better, you are wrong. You will be amazed, at how a weight will lift off of you. Get around others that raise the bar instead of dragging you under it, suffocating you under it's weight.

Over twenty years ago, I decided it was time to make some changes. One of those changes was I would no longer drink. I didn't have a problem with it. I just didn't see a purpose in it anymore. I like to be in control. If you are drunk, or buzzed, you are not in control anymore.

I told one of my "friends" that I was going to quit. He laughed and said I couldn't.

"Oh, I can," I said." I can also get new friends."

Did that hurt a little? You bet. I thought we were good friends. I expected a bit of encouragement. I got none of that. He didn't love or care about my goals.

Within a few months of that, I met a new group of people. They didn't drink but they were fun to hang around. They made me laugh. They had dreams. I had dreams. We all pushed each other. People that care about the betterment of their fellow man love them. It is that simple.

It is important to be loved. It is important to love others as well. You need to surround yourself with people that not only bring out the best in you and push for you to improve. People that do that, love you.

You need to be with people that have a burning desire towards improvement and growth. You need to be around those that empathize with you. When you feel hurt, they feel hurt with you. You share their pain, triumphs, losses and wins as if they are your own. We may refer to these under different names, but in the end, it is love that drives why we care when they laugh and they cry. It is also love that lifts them up instead of holding them down.

Again, God never intended for us to be alone. He squishes this belief early on in the book of Genesis.

> ### It is not good for man to be alone. I will make a helper suitable for him.
> ### Genesis 2:18 NIV

When my grandmother, Vera Lafever, passed away, her funeral was a reflection of a great woman who lived a life enveloped in love. The room was packed for both services. As I gave the eulogy, I was in awe of the room. It was filled with people coming to show respect for someone they cared for and loved. During the reception, it was nonstop stories from the people coming through the line. They told us things we never knew. She never bragged about the good she did in this world. She never shouted out how great she was. She lived a non-social media life, filled to the brim with social activities, and schedules that had to be kept. It was filled with birthday parties, graduations, hand-written letters, trips to hospital rooms and retirement homes, to sit and chat as well as her weekly card games where she played with the same people for over 50 years.

I knew she was a woman of tremendous love, with a big heart, but didn't know the depths of it until I heard from others what she meant to them. I am not mad that I didn't know these valuable details. I have respect for how she loved without the expectation of it to come back, because she learned something that I didn't understand.

If you love, it will come back. It will come back pressed down and overflowing. It will come back in ways you can never imagine. Love can't help but attract more love.

Love given away has a way of returning to you. My grandma knew this and never hoarded it. She gave it, again and again. I saw the impact of it, what it meant to the people that traveled from across the country to pay their respects.

You must also find love in the simple things outside of your family and close friends.

Love the circumstances of life.

You can look at your job and complain or you can look at it and be thankful you have one. You can be thankful they trust and respect the skill you bring to them. You are there to solve the issues and make that place great. Love that they trust you to do it.

You can look at the traffic jam, and be mad that you are running late, or you can be glad you have a reliable car with a working stereo to sing along as you crawl along. You know you aren't the only one running late so kick back and enjoy the ride. Love the extra "me" time you just got gifted.

Love the challenge of the day. Love the opportunity for growth it brings with it.

Problems above ground are better than no problems six feet under. Love the challenge of finding solutions and failing forward. Love the ability to be better today than you were yesterday. Love the chance to prove your awesomeness.

What about the people that make bad decisions?

People will do you wrong in this world. How do you show them love? How can you find love in the hate that some will throw your way?

Wow. That one is tough. I would be lying, if I said that I have never struggled with this one. Humans have done me wrong in the past. Sometimes, it was by people I knew and thought were my friends. Sometimes, they were by people I didn't know.

Getting hate, from those I didn't know, was easier to take. They didn't know me so I could find reasons to shrug it off. We all know people, that make snap decisions about others, based on little to no facts. In the social media world, we call those people, keyboard warriors. Honestly, they can take their opinion about me, and do with it what they may, because it doesn't affect my day. They haven't entered my circle of trust.

For the people that know me, when they do me wrong, or have misguided hate, that hurts. There is no real way around that.

There is a way, for me to react back, though. It took me years to realize, the best way for me to act back, was not with hatred. Poisoning my own soul and heart with hatred, serves no purpose. At the very least, I need to shrug it off. The better approach is to wish them the best and pray for them.

Again, I would be lying, if I said this was easy. Loving those, who don't love you, is a tough battle with your inner self. It goes against what society would probably advise. That said, since we are looking to be better humans, it would probably be best to take a lot of what society offers as advice with a shovel full of salt.

Finally, you need to love yourself. You can love someone special, your friends, and even people that don't love you back. Now, it is time for you to also love yourself.

This may seem simple on the surface, but for many, it isn't. Many have conversations daily, hourly and even every few minutes, saying how they don't love themselves so why should anyone else love them?

I am here to tell you something. You need to stop listening to those voices. They have no idea what they are talking about. Everything they say, regarding you not being worthy of love, is nothing but pure nonsense.

You need to know that you are worth loving. God makes no junk. He made you in His image! If that is truly the case, which by the way it is, how is it possible that you aren't worthy of love from others as well as yourself?

Do me a favor. When you look in the mirror tonight, tell yourself how awesome you are. Tell yourself you can do anything you set your mind to doing. Let yourself know, that God makes no junk, that you are loved, and that you love who you are and who you will become.

Tomorrow, do me another favor. Say it again. Say it every day until you believe it. Get to the point, where you can walk by the mirror, see yourself, and with a wink and a smile, know that you are loved by yourself, others, and God above.

Find love, embrace love, and never ever let it go. You deserve it and it is your right.

RULE #10) KNOW GOD

"15 For this reason, ever since I heard about your faith in the Lord Jesus and your love for all God's people, 16 I have not stopped giving thanks for you, remembering you in my prayers. 17 I keep asking that the God of our Lord Jesus Christ, the glorious Father, may give you the Spirit of wisdom and revelation, so that you may know him better."
Ephesians 1:15-17 (NIV)

WHY WOULD I, A STRONG believer that Jesus was the Son of God, who died for our sins and rose three days later, put this rule all the way down at #10?

This is exactly what my wife asked me.

That is an excellent question with a very weak answer. I

would love to tell you I have some deep philosophical reasoning behind it but I don't. It is quite simple.

It is Rule #10 because God had a top 10 and yeah...that is why. That is sad, right?

I am no theologian but I know what I believe. Life, without knowing God, is pointless.

Yep. I said it. Pointless. Without meaning. It is a waste of time and energy.

I am going to explain my feelings on God but let's start from a naysayer point of view.

I have heard people claim there is no God. Some will say I am wasting my time believing in a higher power. I must be some kind of religious nutjob, for thinking all of this was created by a supreme being. I definitely had a little extra cuckoo in my corn flakes.

Okay, so how did we get here? The Big Bang Theory?

That's cute...

We can go with that for a moment.

After the big bang, our planet and system just kind of happened. You see, everything blew up and these random carbons floating around decided to unite together to form planets and they all started revolving perfectly around the sun. Every 365 days it just lined up the seasons around the third planet like clockwork. Hey, on top of everything else, let's make the planets spin perfectly on their axis because of this Big Bang.

Well, the planets were a little bare. The third one from the sun, in the Milky Way system, needed stuff on it, So cells, carbon, and elements from that periodic table, kind of did their thing and made random things. You know, stuff like plants, fish, water, air, and eventually people.

HOWEVER, because these cells are so good, they were able to make tens of thousands of different plants, animals, fish and food. I mean, without this Big Bang, none of this is even remotely possible!

The people were interesting. A group here, a group there, all different races and tons of different languages because cells have a sense of humor about what they were making.

Stop...just stop.

Ugh...that all hurts the brain.

So, how did everything REALLY come to exist? God.

How else could it really have happened? All of this, the stars, planets, and everything on them, have to be from one higher being.

I had an atheist say to me, "What if you are wrong?"

My answer was quite simple.

"You are betting everything on there being no God. If you are right, it was all for nothing anyway. If you are wrong, you lost eternity. If I am wrong, it would mean nothing. But, if I am right, are you really willing to risk all of eternity?"

Okay, God exists. Now what?

Our God wants us to know him.

I recommend you start with a few things. The Bible, church, and a group of people to discuss what you are learning.

First, let's talk about the Bible.

Years ago, I didn't know that there existed more than the King James Version. That version is beautiful in its poetic flow and an awesome Bible, but can be quite intimidating to someone when they first pick it up. All of the "thee" and "thou art" talk can be a little intimidating. Wow. I tried and failed to read it many times. I was given a Bible at the church where I grew up. Engraved with my name on the cover, that was still not enough for me to get past reading the red text parts where Jesus spoke.

Sometime in my twenties, someone I admired greatly for their financial success, and how they carried themselves as a person, told me they read the Bible every year from cover to cover. That just blew my mind! I had seen the Bible. It was pretty thick, with tiny print, written in a manner difficult to understand. How was this even possible?

He showed me his Bible and it was a different translation, NIV, the New International Version. I am not saying this is the best of all translations. I can tell you that my "pile of goo brain", was ecstatic to finally have a Bible to read that was in English that I could understand. I have since moved on, and read other translations, but this one was very important to my initial introduction to the Bible.

This Bible had a section in the back that had a reading plan for getting through the Bible in one year. It was a little of this book, a little of that book. I was through the Bible 365 days later.

Do you know why it is important to read the Bible? You really get to know God and what he did for his people. You get to learn about Jesus and the sacrifice he made. You get to see the mistakes and triumphs, the failures and successes, of people throughout the ages.

16 All Scripture is breathed out by God and profitable for teaching, for reproof, for correction, and for training in righteousness, 17 that the man of God may be complete, equipped for every good work.
2 Timothy 3:16-17

The Bible is massive. It can look intimidating. I have a couple suggestions if you have never read it. First, start with the New Testament. If that still feels daunting, then start with the Gospels. Those would be Matthew, Mark, Luke and John.

If that still seems daunting, we live in the age of technology so we are blessed to have the Bible on audio. You can sit back and have somebody read it to you.

Whichever option you choose I recommend you just get started. I decided to read the Bible for one reason. I got tired of people telling me what was in it or not in it. I felt it was best to see for myself. I have now been through the Bible many times, and I can say that I get something new out of it each time. That could be because I feel I am growing in my faith everyday.

People like to point out the failures and the bad stuff in the Bible. After reading it, I learned the meaning behind the failures. In all of the failures and mistakes, of the people in the

Bible, we learn that they weren't perfect. We see that God loved them and in spite of their shortcomings, he continued to love them and welcome them back with open arms. I learned we had a forgiving God, and his Son (Jesus Christ) that died for our sins.

> *5 Trust in the Lord with all your heart,*
>
> *and do not lean on your own understanding.*
>
> *6 In all your ways acknowledge him,*
>
> *and he will make straight your paths.*
>
> *Proverbs 3:5-6*

I wanted to read the Bible so I knew what it said. I still read it completely through once a year.

Some, usually non-believers (but not always), will tell you it isn't relevant today. You can't practice any of it in these 'modern' times.

Check these out:

You shall not steal. Exodus 20:15

Love your neighbor as yourself. Mark 12:31

In everything, then, do to others as you would have them do to you. Mathew 7:12

I love this one:

> *For everything in the world – the lust of the flesh, the lust of the eyes, and the pride of life – comes not from the Father but from the world. The world and its desires pass away, but whoever does the will of God*

lives forever. 1 John 2:16-17

Said another way:

Life is short. Heaven is forever

Reading the Bible does come with some challenges. As I discussed earlier, it comes in many different versions. You have to know the significance of the events happening at that time. Where are all these people and places?

I recommend diving into books about the bible or breaking down different events in the Bible. Really dig deeply into the circumstances of what was going on at those times in history. With this increased knowledge, I feel the impact of the verses more.

Suggesting books or a book that helped me out is tough but if I had to pick one, it would be *The Purpose Driven Life by Rick Warren.* I also like reading autobiographies about people's faith walk, their trials and tribulations. There is a lot of knowledge that can be gained, from seeing others, and how they came to know God.

That brings us to the importance of a church.

"Ugh. Church is boring. I don't like the music. The pastor dresses weird. Why are they giving us wine and crackers? Why do all these people know what to say? Was that taught last week? Do I have to dress up?" Sound familiar?

You know what is great about churches in America? They are everywhere and they come like Baskin Robbins, many different flavors.

A few years ago, I struggled with this one.

Okay, let's be real. I didn't just struggle. I really didn't like to go. I believed in God. I believed Jesus Christ died for my sins. I just didn't want to go to church because it was so boring.

I wasn't clicking with the church. I had gone to boring churches my whole life. Look, sometimes I am perfectly happy singing hymnals. Usually, I need to wake up so I prefer my church to rock out!

I honestly thought I was dreaming of something that didn't exist. A church with guitars, rock music blaring away that touched my soul seemed like the "unicorn." It was all imagination...

One Sunday, my wife dragged me to church. The music wasn't memorable. We had a substitute pastor teaching, or trying to anyway. He was teaching on Job. Now, for those of you that don't know, Job lost everything, his family, his house, his money, his livestock, I mean EVERYTHING. It isn't a quick read to get through the book of Job. It is 42 chapters long. Why did this guy, who was teaching, think he was going to explain it all in 30 minutes? I have no idea.

Well, no surprise, he didn't. I don't even think he made it half way through setting the foundation of the book.

I was floored when he said he was out of time...sorry. His bad.

Look, people are starving for knowledge about the Word of God. I believe people want to know that there is a purpose to all of this.

I call it a faith walk.

The problem is, it is hard to walk when the one leading isn't prepared or planning to lead people in their faith walk.

A great church should excite you past the one hour of attendance every Saturday or Sunday. It should inspire you to go back into the world for the other 167 hours a week with a sense of purpose and a mission.

I have never left church mad. I wasn't just mad. I was pissed-off. I was at a spiritual crossroad. I was studying the Bible. I was reading faith-based books. I was ready to grow more and get to really know God.

"I know you want me to go to church," I said to Melissa. "I agree I need to go to church, but we have got to find one that works for me. I am not inspired to roll out of bed for this. I mean, he couldn't even get through the message. What the eff is that about?"

I am pretty sure I used the word that rhymes with duck...

Yeah, I definitely did.

I said I needed to grow and still do need to grow since I refer to myself as the cursing Christian.

On that day, I had a choice to make. Give up, and stop going all together, rather than sporadically like I was now, or search for a new church. I knew my current struggles were because I needed outside knowledge, and a church to call home, which was a big deal to my growth as a Christian.

Knowing that there were lots of churches, we started church shopping. There is no shame in that. Really. I had a list I wanted to check out. The funny thing is that it was the second one on the list that I clicked with.

I remember walking in and the band was playing The Foo Fighters song, *The Great Pretender*. I was hooked right then. It was loud. The message was relevant. They were talking about events from almost 2000 years ago but making a correlation to people today.

I was in love with MY new church.

Over the next year or so, my wife and I rarely missed a service. They had them on Saturdays and Sundays and even had one that started at noon on Sunday. There really is no excuse in missing that one...

Now, I had two things knocked out. By reading the Bible, I was getting into God's word and getting to know him that way. I still needed some help though, and that was where going to church fit in to things. I was getting the theology along with meaning. The only missing piece was having others to bounce all this off of, so I could get even deeper into the Word.

I needed fellow Christians who I could meet with on a weekly basis to discuss and go deeper into what we had just learned.

A lot of churches have Bible studies. Some are men, or women only, couples, or people with (let's say) more biblical experience (ahem) or young families. I never really understood the purpose of them until our new church told us why they were important.

They called them neighborhood group. You could pick one that was around your neighborhood. They meet once a week and you go over that week's lesson or some other lesson the church has planned.

We had heard about it, and even talked about finding one, but never did anything about our first year at the new church, CCV. Until, one day the phone rang. Melissa said we were invited to one and could check it out and see what we thought.

I don't know what I was expecting. I think I may have been expecting a bunch of holy rollers, being splashed with holy water or something. I was worried because I had so much growing yet to accomplish. I thought, what if they don't accept me? Then what?

Everyone was very inviting and friendly. We chatted for a little while and then dove into the lesson that week. We talked about what it meant, how it impacted us and what we all thought of it. How could we apply the lesson to our lives? It was all about figuring out how to be a better Christian.

It was the third piece, the missing leg of the stool. With all three, I felt I had a solid foundation to my faith walk.

Knowing God isn't something you will figure out or ever understand completely. I need to make sure you understand that.

It is a faith walk. It isn't a faith sit down.

Your journey learning about God will be full of ups as well as downs. You will have days where you will feel like screaming from the rooftops about how awesome our God is. You will also have days where you feel alone and abandoned.

It is a faith walk. Understand that He has a plan. Stay strong and carry on.

I have had my times when I felt he abandoned me and realized later on that what I thought was a bad event actually brought me to where I am.

Our God is an awesome God. He will never give you more than you can handle. Know that he never gives you more than you can handle.

On that note, God really thinks a lot of you are a bad ass with the amount of challenges he throws your way. Count your blessings and be thankful that he trusted you to be an example of how to overcome.

You may be thinking about the unfair things that happen in this world and not understand why our God let's them happen. That's okay. We can't know everything or every reason.

My church brought up a stat today about our attendance. On the surface, we look like a big church. It is the fifth largest church in the country. However, if you take the population of our area, less than 1% of the people attend our church. It is humbling. We are actually a small church then.

So what does that have to do with knowing God?

Think about it this way: Our God is all knowing and all seeing. We want to know him but we will never know all of his ways or reasons. We will know some and have to rely on faith when bad things happen because God always has a plan.

11 For I know the plans I have for you," declares the Lord, "plans to prosper you and not to harm you, plans to give you hope and a future. Jeremiah 29:11

This rule cements the foundation. Without Rule 10: Know God, the others have nothing to stand on and would have less meaning. Knowing God is critically important to keeping a purpose and a reason to every rule covered in this book.

Are you still skeptical? It is your life, but understand that whether you like it or not, you are on a faith walk. It doesn't matter if you are choosing not to participate in it.

Take the skepticism you have and turn it around. What if you are wrong? Would it really hurt you to try and get to know God?

Pick up a Bible, find a church you can connect with others, as well as a bible study group to talk through your concerns and questions. It is time to invite God in and get to know Him.

EPILOGUE

An Open Letter To My Boys

You have made it to the end of this book. It happened one of two ways. One, you skipped to the end, or two, you read it. Either way, here we are.

Some of you aren't yet ready to leave home. That is okay. Look at everything you have read as a guide for when you do. For my oldest, Zachary, my hope in writing this was to put you in the best position possible.

The world will have its challenges, but it is easier when you have a plan.

When I left home, I had little idea of what I was doing. There were vague wants and theories of how to make it less complicated, but I stumbled along the way.

As strange as it may sound, I thank God that I did. Without

the challenges I went through, I know this book would have never come about. Be glad that I took bumps along the way to hopefully save you from some of them.

I will guarantee that you will stumble. I know you will go through some frustrating times and challenges. As much as it makes little sense that I would want you to have these moments, I want you to experience them.

This book is written to make it easier for you, but life without moments and opportunities of growth would be a Pollyanna dream that is simply not possible.

The purpose of the rules in this book is to give you a foundation to fall back on. When the challenges happen, look here and know that I left you a guide to make it easier to get through the tough times.

Dad's got your back.

Treat people with respect. Being a jerk doesn't impress anyone worth impressing. If it does impress someone, you need to get away from them and make new friends.

Make mistakes. Fail. Just, don't be an idiot. If you know something is a bad idea, use your head and don't do it.

Before making a brash decision or saying something hurtful, take a moment to ask yourself if it is worth saying at all. Not every argument is worth having or needing to be won.

Bad things are going to happen. That's life. Get through it and know that tomorrow is another day.

Patience sucks. However, at times it will be unavoidable. Weigh out whether the prize that follows is worth it. If not, go find something where waiting is worth it.

Take the time to study why things went right or wrong. There will always be clues to why things worked out or failed.

Be kind. If someone holds a door for you or smiles, do the polite thing and say, thank you, or smile back.

Relatively speaking, life is short. Don't waste it. If your job stinks, go get another one that is more fulfilling. If you want to go see Paris, don't put it off.

Life isn't meant for you to be alone. Find someone special to love or people with which to enjoy it.

Have a relationship with God. If you know God, and live a life grounded in God, others will take notice. When others notice, the chance of them wanting to know God, change and be better humans is more likely.

Go be a better human. Be the example the world has been waiting for. Go out and set an example so that others will want to human better as well.

Love, Dad

THANK YOU

Have you ever read the "Thank you" section in the liner notes of an album? I often wondered how they remember everyone. Then it hit me that they can't. It is utterly impossible to remember all the people that influence you in the creative process. In saying that, I am going to try my best.

I would like to thank all the moms and dads that I have encountered throughout my life. Whether I saw moments that made me cheer inside at your parenting super powers, or witnessed events out of the Legion of Doom handbook, you influenced me in these writings.

John Kivel, I now know your pain when you do liner notes in albums. Thank you, for the many hours of long talks, and being a true friend and person I can trust. I can't begin to explain the value that added to these pages.

Melville Edward Schwab...if that is your name. I know the trade for your middle name was done fair and square. Thank you for the many years of friendship. I appreciate you tolerating my stories as I have tolerated yours.

I want to thank Nick Trevillian. If not for you, this may still be a dream in my head. You pushed me to meet with a publisher and put my ideas to paper.

Phil Shaver, thank you for being a sounding board over the years and listening to my whacked-out brand of philosophy, whether it was with how I deal with people or clients. God gifted you with patience when it comes to dealing with me.

James Harness, thank you for all your years of wisdom and making me laugh. Who knew that two young punks who met at a Little Caesar's Pizza, shared an apartment and partied at said apartment in our formative years would grow into responsible adults?

Jeremy Jones, thank you for taking a shot on the idea I pitched to you. I look forward to many more years of teaming up for what I hope to be countless books of my...err...wisdom.

My kids, Zachary, Alexander (Bubba), and Jackson. Without you, let's be honest, this idea never would have come about. Thank you for making me want to be a better father and motivating me to pass on the wisdom out of the mistakes or stumbles I have had.

Thank you, to my wife, Melissa. It is hard to sum up a thank you, in a paragraph, to someone who has been my partner since we were 19 years old. I think, it is safe to say, that a lot of my growth over the years is due to you. Without you, I cringe at what I may have become.

Lastly, so I forget no one, I want to thank every person that has come in and out of my life. Yep. I know that is somewhat of a copout. With every person that passed through my life, I got something. While some may no longer be in my day-to-day world, I value the memories and the lessons I learned to become a better human.

ABOUT THE AUTHOR

Kevin Belzer was born in Burlington, Iowa decades ago. Up until the age of 33 he moved between Iowa, Illinois and Indiana. At the age of 33, he decided it no longer made sense to live in a place where it got so cold in the winter that you couldn't feel your face. Why would anyone live where they couldn't feel their face?

He has been a Realtor since 2008. It seemed to make the most sense to him that getting into a business while everyone else was fleeing it would be a great idea. He ended up being right.

Kevin currently resides in Anthem, Arizona with his wife, Melissa, and three boys, Zachary, Alexander and Jackson. They also have two awesome cats, Bogey and Piper.

9 781945 849558